VISUAL QUI

PHOTODELUXE 2

FOR WINDOWS AND MACINTOSH

JENNIFER ALSPACH

TED ALSPACH

Peachpit Press

Visual QuickStart Guide

PHOTODELUXE 2

for Windows and Macintosh

Jennifer Alspach
Ted Alspach

Peachpit Press
1249 Eighth Street
Berkeley, CA 94710
(510) 524-2178
(510) 524-2221 (fax)
(800) 283-9444
Find us on the World Wide Web at:
http://www.peachpit.com

Peachpit Press is a division of Addison Wesley Longman

ISBN: 0-201-69670-3

0 9 8 7 6 5 4 3 2 1

Printed and bound in the United States of America

♻ Printed on recycled paper

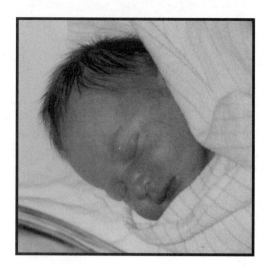

Dedication

This book is dedicated to Gage Xavier Alspach, who arrived just in time to make sure we got a picture of him in the book.

About the Authors

Jennifer Alspach is a nationally reknowned artist and author whose artwork has appeared in a wide variety of publications. She is the author of several books and articles on computer graphics.

Ted Alspach is the author of more than a dozen books on desktop publishing and graphics, as well as hundreds of articles on related topics. His books have been translated into more than a dozen different languages worldwide.

Jennifer and Ted are the owners of Bezier Inc., located somewhere in the middle of Arizona. They have six cats, a dog, a horse, and a Gage.

Feedback

Please send any comments regarding this book to Jennifer and Ted at:

PhotoDeluxeVQS@bezier.com

Other books by Jennifer Alspach

Photoshop and Illustrator Studio Secrets

Illustrator 7 Complete

Illustrator Filter Finesse

Microsoft Bob (we were duped into writing it)

Other books by Ted Alspach

Illustrator 7 Studio Secrets

PageMaker 6.5 for Windows: Visual QuickStart Guide

PageMaker 6.5 for Macintosh: Visual QuickStart Guide

Illustrator 7 Bible

Acrobat 3 for Macintosh and Windows: Visual QuickStart Guide

Photoshop 4 Complete

KPT Studio Secrets

Macworld Illustrator 6 Bible

Illustrator Filter Finesse

The Mac Internet Tour Guide, 2nd Ed.

Microsoft Bob (it was Jen's idea, honest)

Internet E-mail Quick Tour

The Complete Idiot's Guide to Photoshop

The Complete Idiot's Guide to QuarkXPress

Macworld Illustrator 5.0/5.5 Bible

Acknowledgements

Many individuals contributed to this book in some way or another:

Nancy Davis, our incredible editor at Peachpit.

Scott Calamar at LightSpeed Publishing.

The Taylors, who tested everything with an amazing amount of enthusiasm and accuracy.

All of the wonderful subjects in the photographs, including: Jerry, Yote, Opa, Toulouse, Carol A, Michelle, Cathy, Morgan, Murphy, Sage, Static, Jim, Jackie, Leena, Linus, C.J., Nelson, Bernice, Carol G, Pierre, Harvey, Diane, Minnie, Lee, Jimmy, Oma, Sam, and Ken.

And finally, everyone at Peachpit Press who helped move this book along until it hit paper.

Colophon

This book was created using:

Adobe PhotoDeluxe 2.0

QuarkXPress 3.32

Extensis QX-Tools 2.0

Adobe Photoshop 4.0.1

Flash-It! 3.0.2

Adobe Illustrator 7.0.1

Extensis VectorTools 2.0

Pentium 200/MMX with Windows 95

PowerCenter 180

UMAX S900L/200

Adobe Garamond was used for the body copy, and Futura Extra Black Condensed was used to create the headings. VAG Rounded was used for the chapter titles and folios.

Book Design: Ted Alspach

Editor: Nancy Davis

Copy Editor: Scott Calamar, LightSpeed Publishing

Technical Editors: Diane and Ross Taylor

Index: Rebecca Plunkett

TABLE OF CONTENTS

3 • Guided Activities

4 • Selection Techniques

Table of Contents

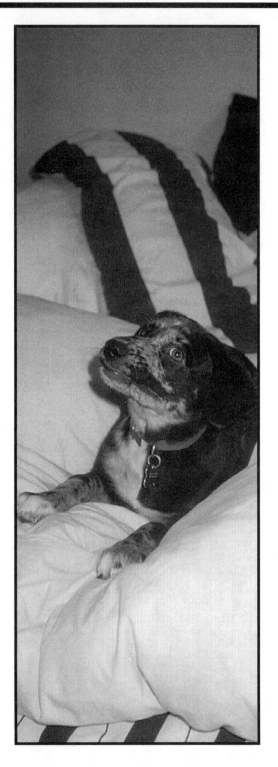

Table of Contents

Table of Contents

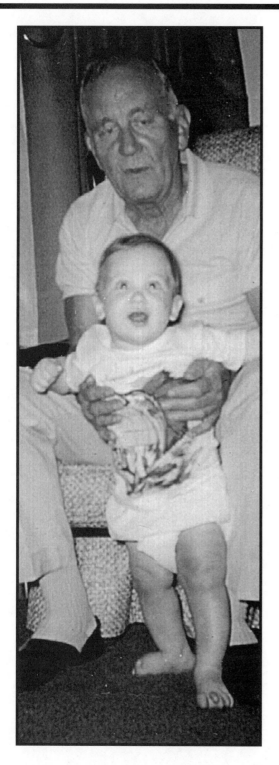

Keyboard Shortcuts

Table of Contents

INTRODUCTION

Adobe PhotoDeluxe is the most popular image editing software available, with millions of copies floating around the world. PhotoDeluxe 2.0 allows you to accomplish amazing things with photographs, from making a terrible image look respectable to making a good image look incredible. The editing and photo manipulation capabilities of the software allow you to quickly and easily put Rex's tail on mom, add lightning from one photo to the sky behind your house, and much, much more.

It's easy to be intimidated by PhotoDeluxe's vast array of buttons and tabs. Even if you have some idea of what you're supposed to be doing, just finding the correct function can be an exercise in futility.

That's where this book comes in handy. It covers the most common tasks that you'll want to take on in PhotoDeluxe, along with some useful techniques that you might not even have imagined. Each task is presented in the most basic format possible, so newbies to both computers and PhotoDeluxe can read each step and refer to the accompanying figure. Experts can quickly skim the text looking for just the information they need. Teachers can use this book as their students follow along, step by step, with each technique.

How to use this book

If you've never used a Visual QuickStart Guide from Peachpit Press (of which there are dozens, covering every major software package), then you'll be pleasantly surprised. This book takes you on a whirlwind tour of PhotoDeluxe 2.0, in a format that is both easy to understand, and fun to read. Examples are presented so you can follow along on your computer, comparing what you see on screen to the pictures on each page. The book is designed so that if you were to read it from front to back, you could do so without having to do any flipping or cross referencing.

Most of the examples are presented in the following fashion:

To work through an example:

1. **Find the appropriate topic in the table of contents, the index, or by flipping through the pages looking at the thumb tabs.**

    The bold text (above) tells you what to do. The regular text below it (what you're reading right now) tells you what happens when you do it, or offers supplementary information you may find useful.

2. **Go to the page where the example appears.**

    I've kept the page numbers nice and big in the lower-outside corner of each page to make finding topics easier.

3. **Read that example's steps.**

4. **At your computer, go through the steps one by one, following the directions on each page.**

    Most of the pages contain just one task with several photographs and screenshots. The pages before and after each example contain related topics that you might find helpful.

The Color Section

If you thumb through this book, you'll run across some full color pages. We would love to have made the entire book full color, but to keep the price of the book at a reasonable rate, we've been allotted only eight color pages.

Fortunately, we've used these color pages to their maximum potential, to show you how PhotoDeluxe works with color images. One thing you'll notice here is exactly what PhotoDeluxe can and can't do; some images are so bad to start out with that PhotoDeluxe merely makes them acceptable. Other images can be made to look stunning in PhotoDeluxe, and we've included a few of those images as well.

PhotoDeluxe is fun

One of the real treats about writing this book was that we were able to do all sorts of things to images that had previously been lying around in dusty photo albums. In fact, this entire book could be looked at as a mass market attempt to publish our photographs...

But of course, it isn't. We tried to present the material in the same ways that most people would use the software: to make images look better and to have fun with photos. We certainly had a lot of fun, doing all sorts of wacky things like placing animal heads on people and changing eye colors. Sure, that's not the most useful or productive thing you can do with PhotoDeluxe, but it's things like that that we've found ourselves (and everyone else who has PhotoDeluxe) doing with the software. Have Fun!

INSTALLATION

THE first thing you'll need to do before using PhotoDeluxe is to install it. Installation for PhotoDeluxe (like most Adobe products) is quite straightforward, although there are a few areas which could potentially cause problems.

This chapter takes you step by step through the installation process, separately for Windows and Macintosh users.

Now that you've gotten your hands on this fantastic program, you need to install it on your computer before you can sit down and "play." Your system needs to meet the minimum requirements before you install.

Adobe PhotoDeluxe System requirements for Windows:

- You'll need a 486 or Pentium processor.

- You'll need Windows 95 (or later) or Windows NT 4.0 (or later).

- 16 megabytes of RAM.

- 45 megabytes of empty hard disk space.

- CD-ROM drive.

- A color monitor with at least a 256 color display.

- Built-in video or a video card that can display 640 × 480 resolution or more in 256 color mode.

Adobe PhotoDeluxe System requirements for Macintosh:

- You'll need a 68040 or PowerPC processor.

- You'll need system software 7.0 or later.

- 16 megabytes of RAM.

- 45 megabytes of empty hard disk space.

- CD-ROM drive.

- A color monitor with at least a 256 color display.

- Built-in video or a video card that can display 640 × 480 resolution or more in 256 color mode.

Systems Requirements

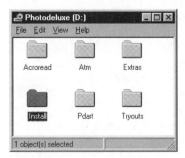

Figure 1. Double-click on the Install folder to open the folder.

Figure 2. Double-click on the Setup icon to launch Adobe PhotoDeluxe 2.0 Setup.

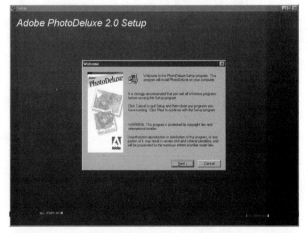

Figure 3. The Adobe PhotoDeluxe 2.0 Setup screen for Windows.

To install Adobe PhotoDeluxe on Windows 95:

1. Insert the PhotoDeluxe CD in the CD-ROM drive.

2. Double-click on My Computer.

3. Double-click on the PhotoDeluxe CD-ROM drive [D:].

4. Double-click on the Install folder to open it (Figure 1).

5. Double-click on the Setup icon (Figure 2).

   This will launch Adobe PhotoDeluxe 2.0 Setup (Figure 3).

6. Click the Next button after reading the information in the Setup screen.

Installation for Windows

TIPS & TECHNIQUES

If Windows 95 is set to auto-run CD-ROMs, the CD will run automatically when inserted in the CD-ROM drive, and present the window shown in Figure 1.

3

7. From the Setup Type screen, choose the type of setup you would like for PhotoDeluxe. (Figure 4).

   For a first installation, we recommend that you choose the Typical install so that all of the components of PhotoDeluxe will be loaded.

8. Click the Next button.

9. In the User Information screen, enter whether you are a business or an individual.

   A good rule of thumb is how you answer your phone. If you say "hello," then you're an individual. If you say something like, "Welcome to Northern Fiduciary Chemical Incorporated," then you're probably a business.

10. Enter your Title/Salutation, First Name, Last Name, Company, and Serial Number in the spaces provided (Figure 5), then click the Next button.

    Adobe PhotoDeluxe's serial number is found on the CD-ROM envelope and on the registration card.

    A verification screen will appear.

11. Verify the information by clicking Yes or No.

12. Click the Next button in the Start Copying Files dialog box.

13. At the next screen, you can choose which Internet components will be installed by clicking the OK button and letting the default components be loaded.

    Depending on your computer and CD-ROM drive, the PhotoDeluxe 2.0 installation process takes about three to five minutes.

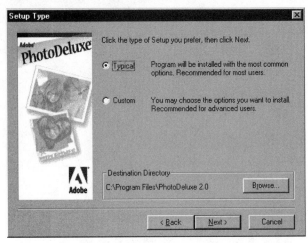

Figure 4. Choose Typical unless you're an experienced user.

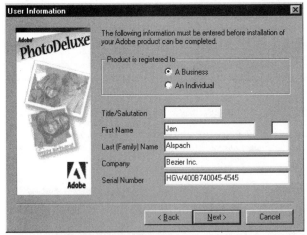

Figure 5. Enter information about yourself in the spaces provided.

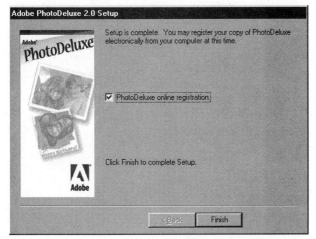

Figure 6. To complete the installation, click the Finish button.

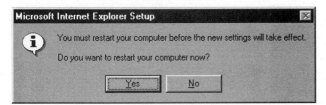

Figure 7. Click the Yes button to have your computer restart automatically when the installation is complete.

14. Click the Finish button to complete the setup and move to the registration screen (Figure 6).

15. You can fill out the registration now, or if you want to get started uncheck the PhotoDeluxe online registration and then click the Finish button.

16. The final dialog box will tell you that you need to restart for the new settings to take effect. Click Yes if you want to restart your computer now or No if you want to proceed with additional installations (Figure 7).

17. Click the OK button and Windows will restart your system.

To install Adobe PhotoDeluxe on a Macintosh:

1. Insert the PhotoDeluxe CD in the CD-ROM drive.

   The CD-ROM will appear on your desktop.

2. Double-click on the PhotoDeluxe CD.

3. Double-click on the Install icon.

   The installation process will continue, with PhotoDeluxe being installed on your hard drive automatically.

Installation for Windows/Macintosh

Launching PhotoDeluxe can be done in various ways.

To start PhotoDeluxe using the Windows 95 Start menu:

Choose Start⮑Programs⮑Adobe⮑ PhotoDeluxe 2.0⮑Adobe PhotoDeluxe 2.0 (Figure 8).

This will start Adobe PhotoDeluxe 2.0. Depending on your choices when you install PhotoDeluxe, your Start menu may be configured differently.

To start PhotoDeluxe by double-clicking an icon:

1. Double-click My Computer.

2. Double-click the C drive.

3. Double-click the Programs File folder.

4. Double-click the PhotoDeluxe 2.0 folder.

5. Double-click the PhotoDeluxe icon.

   This will start Adobe PhotoDeluxe 2.0.

To start PhotoDeluxe on a Macintosh:

1. Double-click on your hard drive.

2. Double-click on the Adobe PhotoDeluxe 2.0 folder

3. Double-click on the Adobe PhotoDeluxe 2.0 icon.

To quit PhotoDeluxe in Windows 95:

Choose File⮑Exit (Ctrl+Q).

To quit PhotoDeluxe on a Macintosh:

Choose File⮑Quit (Command-Q).

Figure 8. *Choose Adobe PhotoDeluxe from the Start menu.*

PhotoDeluxe Basics

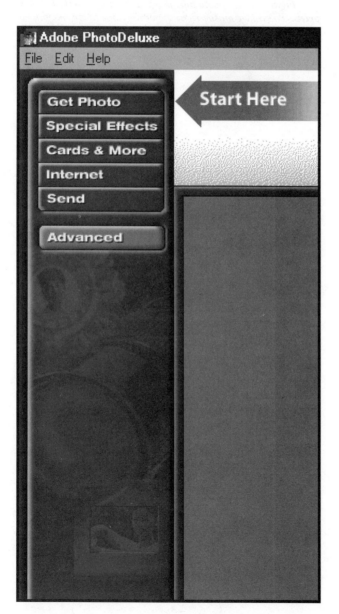

ADOBE PhotoDeluxe is the easiest way to get started in the area of image processing—the art of manipulating photographs in any number of ways. PhotoDeluxe provides all the tools you need to create some truly outstanding effects, as well as to correct existing images.

PhotoDeluxe caters to anyone who has ever been intimidated by powerful, complex software by providing something called "Guided Activities." These activities take you step by step through various procedures, explaining what to do and when to do it. (Guided activities are covered in depth in Chapter 3.)

But beyond the guided activities, there are many other things that you can do to your images, from jazzing up the color to replacing your Aunt Sophie's head with a jack-o'-lantern. This chapter is an introduction to the way PhotoDeluxe works, and how all of the elements and tools tie together to allow you to create extraordinary images right on your computer.

Pixel-based images

Pixelized image is a technical way of saying "photo." When you scan in a photo, the computer reads the information and displays dots (or pixels) on your computer screen. The process of scanning in a photo is also called digitizing. When you see your photo at full size (100%), the pixels are invisible because they are so small that they blend into each other. If you view the photo at a higher magnification, then you'll see the actual pixels (**Figure 1**).

Resolution

Resolution is the number of pixels (dots on your screen) per inch (known as ppi). The higher the resolution, the clearer the image will be (**Figure 2**). If the resolution is low, at full size the photo looks choppy and you can see the actual pixels (**Figure 3**). When you scan in the photo, you set the resolution you want with your scanning software. The resolution also determines the size of the file. A high-resolution photo will create a larger file than a low-resolution photo.

Figure 1. The photo on the left shows the smooth, blended pixels. The image on the right shows the same photo, magnified to see the individual pixels.

Figure 2. This photo shows an image at 300 ppi resolution (high quality).

Figure 3. This photo shows the same image at 72 ppi resolution (low quality).

Pixels and Resolution

TIPS & TECHNIQUES

For viewing a photo on a Web page, your resolution need not be any higher than 72 pixels per inch since all monitors only view at 72 ppi. This holds true for creating photos for on screen presentations.

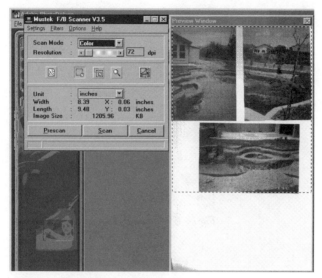

Figure 4. The scanner's software program showing the selection (the dotted line) around the image.

Figure 5. The scanned image will be displayed in PhotoDeluxe for you to work with.

Scanning

Scanning is one of the ways you can get a photo into PhotoDeluxe. You can scan directly using your scanner software, or you can scan from within PhotoDeluxe.

To scan from within PhotoDeluxe:

1. Click the Get Photo button.

2. Click the Scanners button.

3. Choose your scanner.

   This will bring up your scanning software, such as DeskScan, but when you click the Final button, the image will show up in PhotoDeluxe.

4. Select the portion of the image you want to scan using your scanning software's selection tools. (Figure 4).

5. Press Final (or OK, depending on your scanning software).

   The image will now be displayed in PhotoDeluxe (**Figure 5**).

TIPS & TECHNIQUES

If you are printing a file, the resolution of your image will depend on the line screen of your printer. If your image will be used at 100% of its original size, then your image resolution should be two times the line screen's value. A 600 dpi printer has a line screen of 85, which means you would set your resolution to 170 ppi for the image. A 1200 ppi printer has a line screen of 105 so you'd set the resolution to 210 for the image. A 2400 dpi printer has a line screen of 133, which means your resolution would be set to 266.

Scanning

9

Sample images

Another way to get an image into PhotoDeluxe is to use the sample images within PhotoDeluxe, clip art, or a CD with photos. If you are connected to a modem, you can get photos from the Internet.

PhotoDeluxe comes with a good range of photos to get you started. To access PhotoDeluxe's sample photos, simply click on the Sample Photos button (In the Get Photo tab which appears when you click the Get Photo button). The Samples palette will pop up. There are six areas to choose from: Backgrounds, Nature, People, Props, Scenes, and Things.

To see thumbnails of the images:

1. Click the tab of the type of photo you want to view in the Samples palette.

2. Scroll down through the photos or make the palette larger by dragging the lower right corner (Figure 6).

3. Once you find the image you want to use, double-click that image.

   This brings the image into PhotoDeluxe (**Figure 7**).

Clip art

Clip art is art that was drawn in an illustration type program like Adobe Illustrator, then saved so you can use it in many different programs. Clip art can come on a CD, from another application, or you can use PhotoDeluxe's Clip Art samples.

To use PhotoDeluxe's Clip Art:

Click on the Clip Art Button in the Get Photo area of PhotoDeluxe

   The Clip Art palette appears (**Figure 8**).

Figure 6. The Samples palette, showing the thumbnail view of the images.

Figure 7. The image is displayed in PhotoDeluxe.

Figure 8. The Clip Art palette showing PhotoDeluxe's sample clip art.

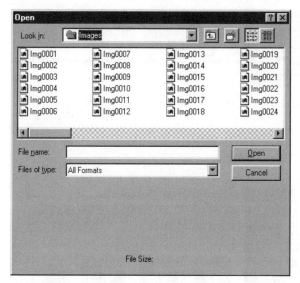

Figure 9. A photo CD's image list is shown here.

Figure 10. Click on this button to access a digital camera's images.

TIPS & TECHNIQUES

Those family photos can easily be put on a CD or a disk by many different companies. Some grocery store and department stores offer this great way to store and use your photos.

CD images

The CD is becoming the most popular way to access a multitude of photos. CDs can be ordered through computer magazines or bought at your nearest computer store. The photos that come on the CD are usually royalty free, meaning that you can use them freely in your own artistic endeavors. Accessing a CD from PhotoDeluxe is a breeze. After clicking the Get Photo button, choose Disc-CD, then choose the photo you wish to use (**Figure 9**).

Digital cameras

A digital camera is a great way to by-pass the whole film development process. With a digital camera, you can take pictures and use them right in PhotoDeluxe without scanning or using a CD. To use images from your digital camera, you must place the digital camera's plug-in module in Adobe PhotoDeluxe's Acquire/Export folder. That way, PhotoDeluxe can read the camera's setup. Then you attach the camera to your computer and click the Cameras button (**Figure 10**).

Copyright infringement

Copyright laws protect the artist who created an image. What this means to you and me is that when a piece of art is copyrighted, you cannot in any way use the whole or even a portion of the art, unless granted written permission by the original artist. When you purchase a CD with a collection of photos, you have to check the licensing agreement regarding how many times you can use the images. Some of the CD collections allow unlimited use of the images. The best rule of thumb is if you are wondering about a certain image, don't use it.

CDs, Digital Cameras, and Copyrights

Buttons for Guided Activities

There are six buttons in PhotoDeluxe that take you through the guided activities. The first button is Get Photo, because you can't do anything without having a photo to start with. With Get Photo, you can access the following: My Photo, Sample Photos, Clip Art, Open File, Cameras, Scanners, Disc-CD, Internet, and Other (**Figure 11**).

The next button is Special Effects. This is where you can have so much fun. The special effects available are: Art, Fun, Collage, Cool, and Cooler (**Figure 12**). The Intro tab explains what each special effect can do. Within each Special Effect there are six or seven effects you can choose from.

With Cards & More, you can create Cards & Calendars, Pages, Labels, and Frames & More (**Figure 13**). Cards & Calendars lets you create calendars, greeting cards, business cards, and sports cards. With Pages, you can make a photo album, signs, covers, certificates, and stationery. Labels lets you create labels, bookplates, cassette labels, and gift tags. Creating a frame or a T-shirt transfer is easy with Frames & More.

Figure 11. The Get Photo button gives you all your options to bring photos into PhotoDeluxe.

Figure 12. Click here to create guided special effects.

Figure 13. Choose this button to create cards and more.

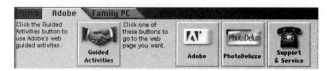

Figure 14. Click here to access the Internet.

Figure 15. To send or print a file, choose the Send button.

Figure 16. To create effects on your own, choose the Advanced button.

The Internet button takes you to the Internet with the click of a button. You have the choice of going to Adobe's web guided activities, Adobe's web page, PhotoDeluxe's web page, Support & Service, or Family PC's web guided activities or Family PC's web page (**Figure 14**). Connecting to the Internet is easy as long as you have a modem and a phone line.

The Send button lets you choose how you want to get your photos out of PhotoDeluxe. You can send a photo to a disk, to the Internet, or to the printer (**Figure 15**).

The Advanced button lets you do activities unguided, free, and on your own. There are six areas in the Advanced section: Edit, Tools, Orientation, Size, Quality, and Effects (**Figure 16**).You can combine an advanced effect with a guided activity. The nice thing about PhotoDeluxe is the ability to combine effects and activities.

For more detailed information on the guided activities, see Chapter 3: Using Guided Activities.

Guided Activity Buttons

PhotoDeluxe Help

With Adobe PhotoDeluxe, you are never alone. There is always a menu available to offer help on specific subjects. The help topics include a Contents tab, an Index tab, and a Find tab.

The Contents tab enables you to click on a specific "book" to get more information on that subject (**Figure 17**). The different books include: PhotoDeluxe Basics; Getting a photo into Adobe PhotoDeluxe; Getting a photo out of Adobe PhotoDeluxe; Organizing your photos; Making a selection; Working with layers; Editing a photo; Painting and editing tools, Resizing and orientation; Adjusting the quality of a photo; Using special effects; Commands; and Troubleshooting. Choose a book by double-clicking on it or by selecting the book and choosing open. Opening a book will display pages underneath the topic (**Figure 18**). Double-clicking on a page will open up the information for your perusal (**Figure 19**).

The Index tab will display all of the available choices that you can receive help on. These choices are listed alphabetically and you can type in the first few letters of the area you are looking for. Think of it as using the index in the back of a book.

The Find tab will bring up a Find dialog box that lets you type in the word(s) you want to find. The Find dialog box will then display all of the available topics on that particular word.

Figure 17. This figure shows the available books to open in the Contents tab.

Figure 18. By double-clicking on a particular book, you'll see the pages in the book.

Figure 19. If you double-click on a page, you'll see the information on that particular topic.

Figure 20. Intro tabs explain a specific activity.

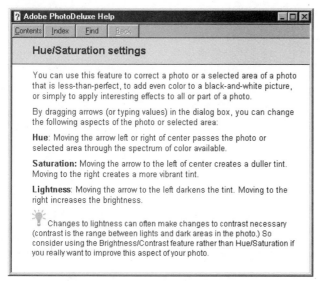

Figure 21. PhotoDeluxe Help showing a square help button step.

Figure 22. The Status Bar shows the size of the current photo in saved file size (372K) and current size (496K). The current size is usually bigger becase it contains data that will be removed when the image is saved.

Intro tabs

Introduction tabs explain how each guided activity works. when you click a button, an intro tab is is displayed. The intro tabs just briefly explain what are contained in each of the guided activity tabs. To get more information on each tab, click on the tab itself and you'll get more detail step by step (**Figure 20**).

Clue cards and Help buttons

Clue cards will pop-up to give you help on certain activities. You can turn these clue cards off if you get tired of seeing these helpful hints. There are two types of Help buttons, square ones and an ever-present round one. The square Help button appears as a rectangle with a question mark in it in individual guided activities on certain steps. When you click on the square Help button, the Adobe PhotoDeluxe Help window comes up to explain what that specific effect will do. (**Figure 21**). The round Help button appears in the toolbar at the top of the photo window. The button looks like a question mark in a circle. When you click on this button the Help menu appears. For more on PhotoDeluxe Help see previous pages in this chapter.

Status Bar

The Status Bar is at the bottom of the PhotoDeluxe screen. This bar shows you the size of the photo (**Figure 22**). If you press and hold the arrow to the right of the status value, you can choose between the Document Sizes, Scratch Sizes (how much room is being used on the hard drive to allow PhotoDeluxe to work with the image), or Efficiency (what percentage of the image is on the hard drive, where lower is better).

Toolbar and photo organizer

The toolbar is found at the top of the window where the photo is located (**Figure 23**). The toolbar has a Zoom Out button, Zoom In button, Zoom tool, Zoom menu, trash can, Object Order button, Text tool, Help button, and Undo button. Zoom In magnifies a photo. Zoom Out reduces the photo's view. The Zoom tool lets you drag a marquee around an area that you want to magnify. The zoom menu gives you a pop-up menu of magnification choices. The trash can deletes any selected object. The Object Order button arranges the order of the objects in the photo. The Text tool enables you to add text to an image. The Help button accesses the online help. The Undo button will undo the last action done to the photo. The Undo button only undoes the very last action you performed.

The photo organizer lets you create your own tabbed galleries of photos. You create your own collection of clip art, sample photos, scanned photos, or photo CDs. To access the photo organizer, click on the My Photos button in the Get Photo guided activity.

Figure 23. The toolbar is found at the top of the Photo window.

The Toolbar and Photo Organizer

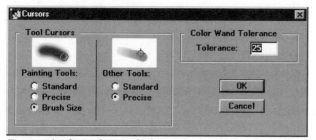

Figure 24. The Preferences for how cursors work in PhotoDeluxe.

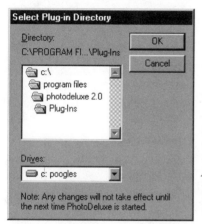

Figure 25. The plug-in directory dialog box. If PhotoDeluxe is pointing to the wrong Plug-in Directory, many tools and filters will not load.

Preferences

PhotoDeluxe has a few preferences to choose from. There are Clue Cards which pop-up to offer help. After a couple of days of seeing the Clue Cards, you may want to turn off that feature. An important feature is to be able to use multiple documents. That way you can have more than one file open at a time. To make multiple documents available, simply check the Allow Multiple Document Windows preference.

The Cursors preference lets you choose options for Painting Tools, Other Tools, and Color Wand Tolerance (**Figure 24**). If you add any third party plug-ins to PhotoDeluxe, you'll need to select the Plug-Ins folder from your preferences (**Figure 25**). The Background preference lets you choose the size and color of your background (**Figure 26**). The Units preference lets you choose the ruler units, Point/Pica Size, and Column Size.

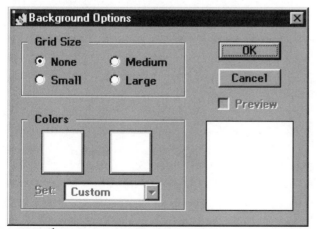

Figure 26. Background Options let you set the size and color of a background grid for your images.

GUIDED ACTIVITIES

GUIDED Activities in PhotoDeluxe take you step by step through each of the tasks you can do. It's handholding that makes a difference; by clicking on successive tabs, you can quickly and easily create almost any effect.

This chapter takes you through the Guided Activity process, and illustrates what happens when you follow a number of the guided activities. Some of these activities are as simple as clicking a button; others take almost a dozen steps to create.

The folks at Adobe tried to create guided activities for the things you'd be doing the most often with PhotoDeluxe. Other procedures can be accomplished using the Advanced button features, which are discussed in Chapter 5 and beyond.

Get Photo

Before starting any PhotoDeluxe activity, an image needs to be opened. PhotoDeluxe offers a variety of ways to get a photo on your screen.

To access Get Photo:

Click on the button called Get Photo, located in the Guided Activities section on the left side of the PhotoDeluxe screen (Figure 1).

The choices for getting a photo are: My Photos, Sample Photos, Clip Art, Open File, Cameras, Scanners, Disc-CD, Internet, and Other.

My Photos are a collection of images that you construct for easy retrieval. When you click on the My Photos button, a window opens. You simply drag a photo you've opened in PhotoDeluxe to the My Photos window and it is saved.

Sample Photos and Clip Art are the images that come with PhotoDeluxe.

Open File will take you to your computer's hard drive to locate a saved image.

When you choose Cameras, Scanner, or Other, you'll have to select the type of camera, scanner, or other input source (**Figure 2**).

If you choose Disc-CD you'll go to an Open dialog box (**Figure 3**) to choose the file type, an appropriate drive, and select an image from a Disc or CD.

When you choose Internet, you'll have to choose your input source, then locate the image that you want to access on the Internet.

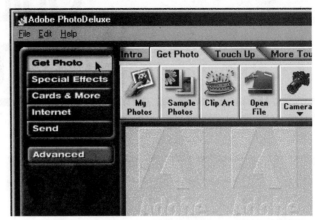

Figure 1. Click on the Get Photo button to access the Get Photo choices.

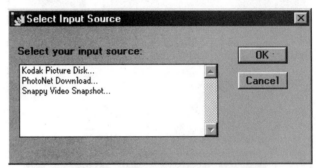

Figure 2. Click on the input sources of your choice.

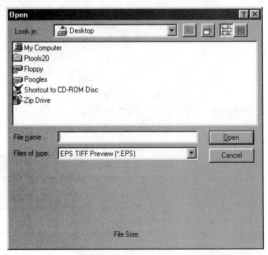

Figure 3. This figure shows the window where you'll choose the drive to access your images.

Bringing Images into PhotoDeluxe

Figure 4. The Sample Photos organizer window enables you to easily access stock images.

Figure 5. The Clip Art organizer window gives a thumbnail preview of the available art.

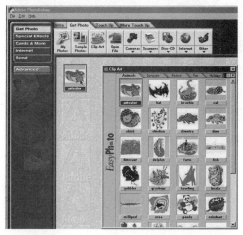

Figure 6. You can drag and drop the image from the organizer window to the PhotoDeluxe window.

To get a photo from Sample Photos or Clip Art:

1. Place the PhotoDeluxe CD in the CD-ROM drive.

2. Click the Get Photo button.

3. Click the Get Photo tab.

4. Click the Sample Photos or Clip Art button.

    A collection of images will appear in a window called the photo organizer window (**Figure 4 and Figure 5**).

5. You can double-click on the image you want, or click and drag the image from the organizer window to the PhotoDeluxe window (**Figure 6**).

    You can leave the Sample Photo and Clip Art organizers up the whole time you are working in PhotoDeluxe. That way you can easily access images with the click of a button.

Sample Photos/Clip Art

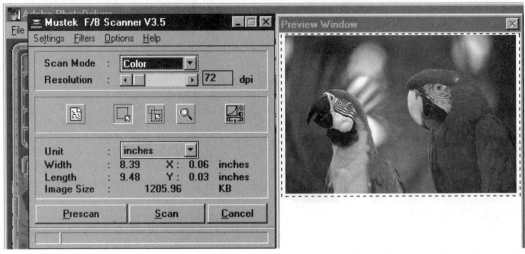

Figure 7. In the Preview Window you can adjust how much of your image you'll scan in.

To bring an image into PhotoDeluxe with a scanner:

1. Click the Scanners button.

2. Click on the name of your attached scanner.

3. Check your image in the scanner's Preview screen (Figure 7).

4. Click on the Scan (or Final) button to see the scanned image in the PhotoDeluxe window (Figure 8).

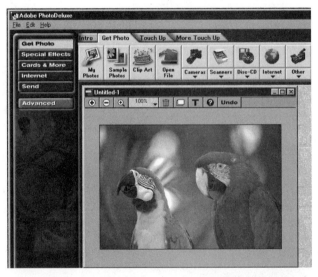

Figure 8. The final scanned image will show up in the PhotoDeluxe window.

TIPS & TECHNIQUES

Keep in mind the final resolution of your image and where the final image will be printed. If you are enlarging or reducing the image, adjust the resolution of your scan when you scan in your image. For more on scanning and resolution, see Chapter 2: PhotoDeluxe Basics.

Figure 9. The original image from a bad photo is gray and unclear.

Figure 10. The Instant Fix button automatically clears up the fuzzy photo.

Touch Up

The Touch Up tab is one of the Get Photo button tabs. The touch ups you can do are: Instant Fix, Size Orientation, Fix Color, Remove Red Eye, and Color Eye. These guided activities take you through each touch up step by step. Some steps are as easy as clicking one button.

To instantly fix an image:

1. Open the photo you wish to fix (Figure 9).

2. Click the Touch Up tab to activate the touch up activities.

3. Click the Instant Fix button and the image will be fixed...er, instantly (Figure 10).

   Some changes will be more subtle or dramatic than others. This feature takes the guesswork out of fixing an image. You may always want to apply Instant Fix to an image to see if it could look any better. You can also combine effects later on when you are more comforatable with PhotoDeluxe.

Touching Up Images

To change the size of an image:

1. Open the photo you want to resize (Figure 11).

2. Click the Size Orientation tab to activate the touch up activities.

3. You need to follow all four steps in order and click on the appropriate responses.

   If you don't want to Adjust, just click the next tab called Trim. If there is no trimming necessary, then click the OK button.

4. Click the Photo Size button to change the size.

   A dialog box will appear asking for the new width and height (Figure 12).

5. Enter the new size for your image and click OK.

6. Click the Done button to complete the activity.

   This will take you back to the Touch Up tabs.

Figure 11. The original photo is ready for resizing.

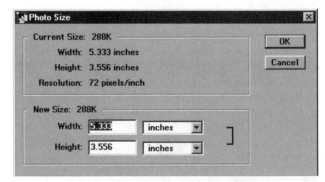

Figure 12. The Photo Size dialog box enables you to enter a new size for your image.

Changing Image Size

Figure 13. This image has too much magenta.

Figure 14. In the Variations dialog box, you can adjust the colors to fix your image.

Figure 15. The image was fixed by adding green and yellow to adjust the color.

To fix the color of an image:

1. Open the image that needs a color fix (Figure 13).

2. Click the Fix Color button.

3. Click the Variations tab.

4. Click the Variations button to apply color changes (Figure 14).

   The Variations dialog box shows you the original and the color that you have changed. You can add Yellow, Red, Magenta, Blue, Cyan, and Green. You can see a thumbnail preview of the changes you are making.

5. Add the opposite color to balance out the image's color.

   Yellow and blue are opposites. Red and cyan are opposites. Magenta and Green are opposites. Add the opposite color to balance out the overpowering color of your image.

6. Click the OK button to accept the new color adjustments (Figure 15).

7. Click the Done tab to return to the Touch Up activities tab.

   You can use Variations to fix an image or to add a whole new twist of color to that image. Dramatically adjusting the colors will create a different look that you may like better than the original.

Color Correction

To remove red eye:

1. Open the image that has red eye (Figure 16).

2. Click the Remove Red Eye button.

3. Click the Select tab.

4. Click the Select Rectangle button.

5. Drag a rectangle around the eyes only (Figure 17).

6. Click the Remove tab.

7. Click the Remove Red Eye button and the eyes are fixed (Figure 18).

8. Click the Done tab to finish the activity.

Figure 16. Red eye is apparent in this image.

Figure 18. The red eye is removed automatically.

Figure 17. Select the area where the red eye occurs.

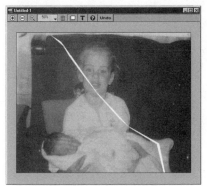

Figure 19. The original old photo has a scratch running through it.

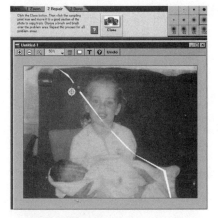

Figure 20. The Clone button enables you to brush away the scratch.

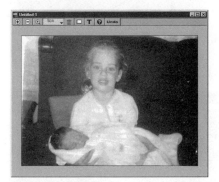

Figure 21. The final image looks like it was never damaged.

To restore an old photo:

1. Open the old photo that needs to be restored (Figure 19).

2. Click the More Touch Up tab.

3. Click the Restore Old Photo button.

4. Click the Zoom tab, then click on the Zoom button to zoom in on the damaged area.

5. Click the Repair button.

6. Click the Clone button.

   The icon changes to the sampling point icon.

7. Move the sampling point icon to a section to copy from.

   PhotoDeluxe memorizes the area you clicked on, and uses that area as a "source" for you to paint with in the following step.

8. Select a brush size and paint away the scratch (Figure 20).

   You'll need to keep moving the sampling point to get a good copy of the image to replace the scratch.

9. Click the Done button to end the activity and see the repaired image (Figure 21).

   The cloning tool also works great as a plastic surgeon's tool. You can easily erase those fine or harsh lines around the eyes and mouth. With PhotoDeluxe, you can take years off of your photos.

Restoring Old Photos

To fix the appearance of an image (instantly making it look better):

1. Open the photo that needs adjustment (Figure 22).

2. Click the More Touch Up tab to access other touch up options.

3. Click the Appearance button.

   The Appearance option lets you clean up an image using Instant Fix, Brightness/Contrast, and Color Balance.

4. Click the Instant Fix tab.

5. Click the Instant Fix button to clear the tones of the image (Figure 23).

6. Click the Tune tab.

7. Click the Brightness/Contrast button to activate the Brightness/Contrast dialog box (Figure 24).

8. Click and drag the adjustment sliders to change brightness and contrast settings.

Figure 22. The original photo needs some drastic adjustment.

Figure 23. The Instant Fix really cleans up the image.

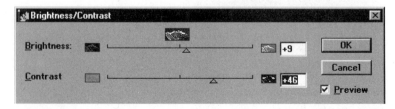

Figure 24. The Brightness/Contrast dialog box provides you with controls to add clarity to the image.

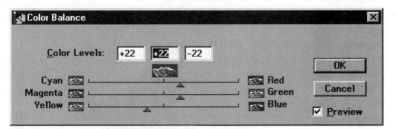

Figure 25. The Color Balance dialog box enables you to fix any overpowering color.

9. Click OK when you achieve the desired effect.

10. Click the Adjust tab.

11. Click the Color Balance button to activate the Color Balance dialog box (Figure 25).

12. Click OK when you create the desired effect.

13. Click the Done button to see the final fixed image (Figure 26).

Figure 26. The final image looks worlds better than the original.

Fixing Image Appearance

29

To create a drop shadow:

1. Open the image that you want to create a drop shadow around (Figure 27).

2. Click the Fun tab in the Special Effects guided activity.

3. Click the Drop Shadow button.

4. Click the Select tab.

5. Click the SmartSelect button.

6. Trace around the edge of your object using the SmartSelect tool (Figure 28).

7. Click when you get back to the start of your trace.

8. Click the Drop Shadow tab.

9. Click the Drop Shadow button to get the Drop Shadow dialog box (Figure 29).

Creating Drop Shadows

Figure 27. The original image needs a shadow to add some depth.

Figure 28. You can see a line when you trace around the edge of your image.

TIPS & TECHNIQUES

When you are tracing with the SmartSelect tool, you can backtrack by moving the cursor backwards and retracing your original path.

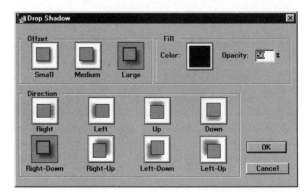

Figure 29. You can choose the type of drop shadow in the Drop Shadow dialog box.

Figure 30. The plain drop shadow looks a little harsh.

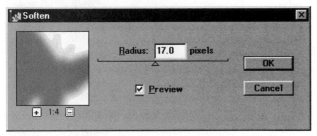

Figure 31. The Soften dialog box gives you a preview of how the shadow will look.

Figure 32. The finished shadow looks soft and natural.

10. **Choose the Offset, Direction, Fill Color, and Fill Opacity.**

    The drop shadow will appear under the selection. (**Figure 30**).

11. **Click the Soften tab.**

12. **Click the Soften button to activate the Soften dialog box (Figure 31).**

13. **Choose the radius and click the OK button.**

    The higher the radius, the softer the edge of the shadow will look.

14. **Click the Done button to finish the activity (Figure 32).**

    Guided activities are a great way to get your feet wet with PhotoDeluxe. You can apply any image to the step by steps you see here. Even the more advanced users of PhotoDeluxe find it easy to use the guided activities to create effects like adding drop shadows.

Creating Drop Shadows

In this exercise, we'll place the head of a cat on the body of a little girl. We know, it's all very B-movie-ish, but it's one of those things *everybody* loves doing with PhotoDeluxe.

To create a collage or body switch:

1. Open the original image from which you want to borrow the head (Figure 33).

2. Click the Collage tab.

3. Click the Body Switch button.

4. Click the Trim tab.

5. Click the SmartSelect button to select the image.

6. Trace around the edge of the cat (or monkey, or person, or whatever) (Figure 34).

7. Click the Delete Background button (Figure 35).

   This removes the background and fills it with white. Don't think of this as beheading animals or people. From experience, the procedure is relatively painless, and the results are worth the effort.

Figure 33. The original image looks fine, but a little PhotoDeluxe manipulation might make it better.

Figure 34. The SmartSelect tool traces wonderfully around the edge of the head.

Figure 35. When you delete the background it will become filled with white, resulting in a decapitated cat in this case.

Collages

Figure 36. When you open the body image, the head automatically gets placed on top.

8. Click the Eraser to remove any background that wasn't deleted.

9. Click the Add Body tab.

10. Open the image with the body you want to use (Figure 36).

11. Click the Resize tab to resize the head to fit the body and drag the head into position (Figure 37).

12. Click the Done button to end the activity (Figure 38).

Figure 37. The Resize tab activates resize lines around the head.

Figure 38. The finished image is completed with no surgery needed.

Collages

Special Effects

The Special Effects guided activities
are where you can have some real fun
with images. There are five categories
of Special Effects: Art, Fun, Collage,
Cool, and Cooler. Within each
category are six or more effects you
can create at the touch of a button.

To create an impressionistic image:

1. Open the image you want to add
   an effect to (Figure 39).

2. Click on the Special Effects
   guided activities button on the
   left side of the PhotoDeluxe
   window.

3. Click the Art tab.

4. Click the Impression button.

5. Click the Crystallize tab.

6. Click the Crystallize button to
   activate the Crystallize dialog box
   (Figure 40).

   The Cell Size slider changes the
   "chunk" size of the crystals that are
   generated using the Crystallize
   filter.

7. Click the OK button to see the
   effect (Figure 41).

8. Click the Done tab to end the
   activity.

Figure 39. The original image to which you want to apply the effect.

Figure 40. When you click the Crystallize button, the Crystallize dialog box opens.

Figure 41. The final image looks great as an impressionistic image.

Figure 42. The original image looks nice, but needs some excitement.

Figure 43. The patchwork dialog box lets you choose the size and depth of the patches.

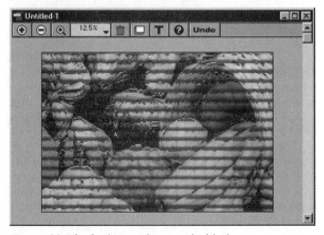

Figure 44. The final image has a quilted look.

To create a patchwork quilt from an image:

1. Open the image you want to patchwork (Figure 42).

2. Click the Cool tab.

3. Click the Patchwork button.

4. Click the Patchwork tab.

5. Click the Patchwork button to bring up the Patchwork dialog box and drag the sliders to adjust the square size and depth (Figure 43).

6. Click the Done button to end the activity (Figure 44).

   Patchwork differs from mosaic because of the shadow and depth it applies to each square. You can make any image look like it was made from a quilt.

Patchwork Quilt Images

35

Cards & More

The Cards & More guided activities let you create Cards and Calendars, Pages, Labels, Frames, and T-shirt transfers. Each activity guides you through creating these effects. At any time, you can access the Help button for assistance.

To create a calendar:

1. Click the Cards & More guided activity button on the left side of your PhotoDeluxe screen.

2. Click the Cards & Calendars tab.

3. Click the Calendars button.

4. Click the Calendar tab.

5. Click the Year button (Figure 45).

6. Click the Year tab.

7. Choose the year you wish. I chose 1998 (Figure 46).

8. Click the Layout tab.

9. Click the Choose Layout button to bring up the Layout Templates (Figure 47).

10. Click the layout you want to use.

    This will bring up a rough layout.

11. Click the Style tab.

12. Click the Choose Style button to activate the Styles Templates (Figure 48).

Figure 45. Click the Year button to create a Year calendar.

Figure 46. Click on the year you want to use when you create a calendar.

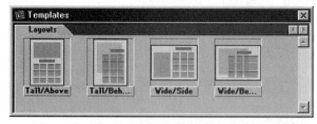

Figure 47. The Layout Templates give you some choices for your calendar layout.

Figure 48. The Styles Templates let you choose the style of the calendar.

Creating Calendars

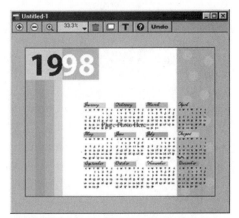

Figure 49. The rough layout is combined with the chosen style.

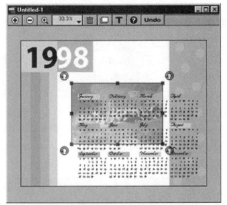

Figure 50. The Resize box enables you to rotate, move and resize an image.

Figure 51. You can use the final image or add more images to it.

13. **Click on the calendar style you wish to use.**

    This will add the chosen style to the rough layout (Figure 49).

14. **Click the Add tab.**

15. **Click on one of the buttons to add your image. I used Open File to retrieve a file I had scanned.**

    This will add the chosen image to the layout.

16. **Resize the image as you wish (Figure 50).**

17. **Click the Done button to end the activity and see the final image (Figure 51).**

    Creating custom calendars can be a great gift for even the most picky friends or relatives. In PhotoDeluxe, you can customize each calendar to even the most discriminating individuals tastes.

Creating Calendars

To create a magazine cover:

1. Click the Pages tab.

2. Click the Covers button.

3. Click the Choose Cover tab.

4. Click the Choose Cover button to bring up the Covers Templates (Figure 52).

5. Double-click on the cover you would like to use as a template.

6. Double-click on the words on the cover to change them (Figure 53).

7. Click on the words to resize, rotate, or move them.

8. Click the Add tab.

9. Click the Open File button to open the photo you want to use.

   The photo appears in the center of the cover. You can resize, move, or rotate it (**Figure 54**).

10. Click the Done button to end the activity (Figure 55).

Figure 52. The Choose Cover button will bring up the Covers Templates.

Figure 53. You can change the text, size, font, and alignment.

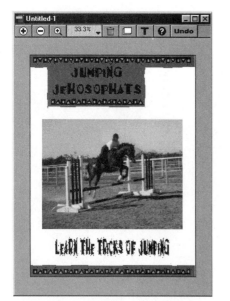

Figure 55. The final cover looks great.

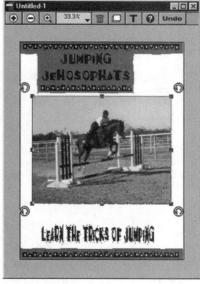

Figure 54. You can move, resize, or rotate your photo.

Figure 56. When you click the Gift Tags button, the Intro explains what you will do.

Figure 57. The Gift Tag templates give you choices for creating gift tags.

Figure 58. The final gift tag is ready for giving.

To create a gift tag:

1. Click the Labels tab.
2. Click the Gift Tags button (Figure 56).
3. Click the Choose Gift Tag tab.
4. Click the Choose Gift Tag button to bring up the Gift Tag template (Figure 57).
5. Click the Add tab.
6. Click the Open File button to add your photo to the tag.

   Once the photo is in place, you can resize, move, or rotate it.
7. Double-click on the text to change the type.
8. Click the Done button to end the activity (Figure 58).

Creating Gift Tags

PhotoDeluxe provides the tools you need to create an image that can be printed to an iron-on transfer (special paper is needed), so that an image can be transfered to a t-shirt.

To create a T-Shirt transfer:

1. Click the Frames & More tab.

2. Click the T-Shirt Transfer button.

3. Click the Choose T-Shirt Transfer tab.

4. Click the Choose Transfer button to bring up the T-Shirts Templates (Figure 59).

5. Double-click on the template you want.

6. Double-click on the type to change it on the template (Figure 60).

7. Click the Add tab to add your photo.

8. Resize the photo if needed.

9. Click the Done tab to end the activity and see the final transfer image (Figure 61).

Figure 59. Click on the template you want to use.

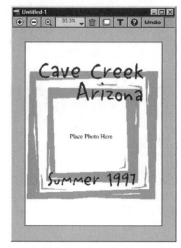

Figure 60. You can change the template type by double-clicking on it.

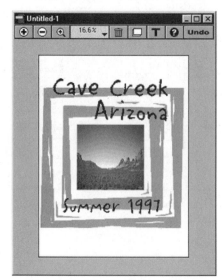

Figure 61. The final image is ready for your T-Shirt transfer.

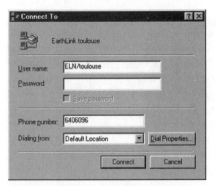

Figure 62. In the Connect To window, you need to enter your name and password.

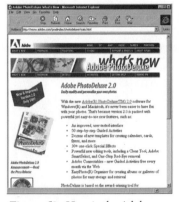

Figure 63. Here is the Adobe PhotoDeluxe web page.

Figure 64. Here is the Family PC web page.

Internet

The Internet guided activity takes you gently through the Internet. This activity takes you through the Adobe web pages, the Family PC web pages, places online to process your photos, and Avery's web pages.

To get to Adobe's PhotoDeluxe web page:

1. Click the Internet button to start the guided activity.

2. Click the Internet tab.

3. Click the PhotoDeluxe button to open your default browser.

   If you aren't currently connected to the Internet, a connection dialog box may appear, such as the one shown in **Figure 62**.

   If you *are* connected, you'll go right to Adobe's PhotoDeluxe page at the www.adobe.com web site.

To get to the Family PC's web page:

1. Click the Internet button to start the guided activity.

2. Click the Internet tab.

3. Click the Family PC button to open your default browser.

   The browser will automatically display the Family PC web page (**Figure 64**).

Internet Access with PhotoDeluxe

Send

The Send guided activity takes you through sending an image to disk, the Internet, or the printer. Each activity has buttons to guide you.

To use the following steps, be sure you have an image open that you would like to print.

To send a file to the printer:

1. Click the Send button to start that guided activity.

2. Click the To Printer tab.

3. Click the Page Setup button to access the Page Setup dialog box (Figure 65).

4. Choose portrait or landscape, your printer, the paper size, and whether you'll use the tray or manually feed the paper.

5. Click the Print Preview button to see the image before it prints (Figure 66).

6. Click the OK button.

7. Click the Print button to bring up the Print dialog box (Figure 67).

   You can access the Page Setup dialog box in the Print dialog box if you click the Setup button.

8. Click the OK button to send your image to the printer.

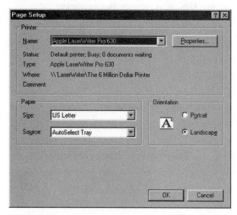

Figure 65. The Page Setup dialog box enables you to change how an image will print.

Figure 66. Print Preview lets you see what the image will look like on your paper size.

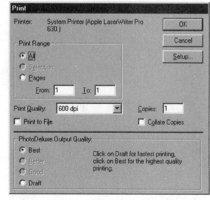

Figure 67. In the Print dialog box, you can set the number of copies to be printed, among other print-related options.

SELECTION TECHNIQUES

THE most important skill to develop when working with PhotoDeluxe is selecting. Selecting is the process of defining a portion of an image to work with, rather than working with the entire image at one time.

PhotoDeluxe provides numerous tools and commands to make the selecting process as straightforward as possible. With so many ways to select, however, it becomes difficult to determine which method is the correct one for any given situation.

This chapter takes you through all the selection techniques and tools one by one, so that you'll understand what each tool does, and when to use it.

Selected areas are indicated by a series of "marching ants," or black and white dashes that circulate around the selected area. Any activities that take place when a selection is active affect *only* the selection.

Making Selections

Before selecting, a Selection tool should be chosen from the Selections palette. The Selection tools are considered an Advanced feature. Selections enable you to affect only a certain section or piece of your image.

When you create a selection around a section of an image, effects are applied to just that selected section. By creating a selection, you can add a drop shadow, blur, spherize, emboss, or many other effects.

To view your selection tools:

1. Click on the Advanced button to get the pull-down menus (**Figure 1**).

2. Choose View⇨Show Selections (**Figure 2**).

   This will display the Selections palette (**Figure 3**).

Figure 1. Click on the Advanced button to access the pull-down menus.

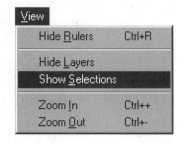

Figure 2. Choose Show Selections from the View menu.

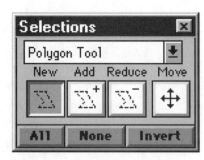

Figure 3. The Selections palette contains all of the tools used for selecting.

TIPS & TECHNIQUES

If a selection exists in the image when you click to create a new selection, the existing selection is deselected and the new selection is made.

To "soften" a selection, choose Effects⇨Feather and type in a small number. This will soften a harsh edge by partially selecting pixels, giving the selection a smoother edge.

Viewing the Selections Palette

Figure 4. The Selections palette pop-up menu shows the nine selection tool choices.

Figure 5. The newly chosen Selection tool's name appears in the description window.

To choose a specific Selection tool from the Selections palette:

1. Display the Selections palette.

2. Choose a Selection tool from the pop-up menu (Figure 4).

   The name of the new Selection tool you have chosen will now appear in the description box of the Selections palette, and the tool itself will appear directly below (**Figure 5**).

The Selections palette

New: Clicking the New button enables you to create a new selection using the current tool. Any existing selection will be deselected when you create a new selection with this tool.

Add: Clicking the Add button and dragging a selection will add the selection to the original selection.

Reduce: Clicking the Reduce button and dragging a selection will delete the selection from the original selection.

Move: Clicking the Move button will move the selection and leave a white "hole" (actually an area filled with white pixels) in the space from where you moved it.

All: Clicking the All button will select everything in that layer. You'll see a box with "marching ants" around the entire image.

None: Clicking the None button will deselect everything in that layer. Any marching ants will disappear.

Invert: Clicking the Invert button will select everything else but what you originally selected.

The Selections Palette

The Selection tools

There are nine selection tools to choose from in PhotoDeluxe. Each tool is used for a specific task (**Figure 6**).

Object Selection tool: The Object Selection tool enables you to move, scale or rotate the whole image without a selection.

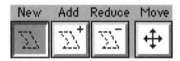

Polygon tool: The Polygon tool creates straight-line polygon selections.

Trace tool: The Trace tool creates freeform selections.

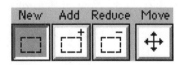

Rectangle tool: The Rectangle tool creates a rectangular selection.

Oval tool: The Oval tool creates oval or elliptical selections.

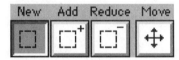

Square tool: The Square tool creates a perfect square selection.

Circle tool: The Circle tool creates a perfect circular selection.

Color Wand: The Color Wand creates a selection of an area that is all the same color.

SmartSelect tool: The SmartSelect tool creates a selection by tracing. The selection will follow an edge formed by different colors.

Figure 6. The nine selection tools in PhotoDeluxe 2.0.

The Selection Tools

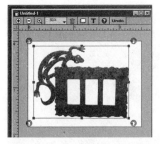

Figure 7. The transformation box is used to move, scale, and rotate selections.

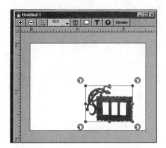

Figure 8. The image after being scaled proportionately.

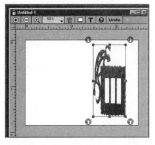

Figure 9. The image scaled horizontally.

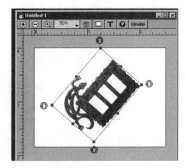

Figure 10. The image rotated freely.

The Object Selection Tool

To transform an image, the Object Selection Tool is the tool to use. It can perform four functions in one shot. The transformations you can perform are: Move, Scale proportionately, Scale disproportionately, or Rotate.

To transform your image:

1. Choose the Object Selection Tool in the Selections Palette.

2. Click one time on the image to display the transformation box (Figure 7).

   The transformation box is a rectangle appearing around the edge of your image with eight points on the corners and along the sides. Circles outside the corners can be used to rotate the selection.

3. Click on a corner point and drag to scale the image proportionately (Figure 8).

4. Click on a vertical middle point to scale the image horizontally (Figure 9).

5. Click and rotate the corner circle to rotate the image freely (Figure 10).

6. Place the cursor in the center of the image and drag to move the image around on the canvas.

   If you want to move the image, put the cursor in the center and drag to a new location. When you have moved, rotated, and scaled the image to your liking, press the Enter key on your keyboard to accept the new changes.

The Object Selection Tool

The Polygon Tool

The Polygon tool creates a straight line shaped selection on the image. By clicking and releasing, you create a straight-lined selection.

To create a polygon-shaped selection:

1. Display the Polygon tool in the pop-up menu of the Selections palette.

2. Choose the New button to create a new selection.

3. Click on the image to create a straight-lined selection.

4. To end the selection, double click with the Polygon tool (Figure 11).

   The Selection tools let you mix and match to make a selection. You can start making a selection with the Polygon tool, then use Color Wand or the Trace tool to add or take away from your selection.

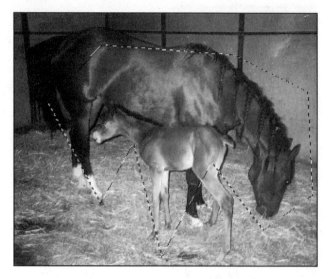

Figure 11. A quick Polygon tool selection has been made around the image.

Selecting Polygonal Shapes

TIPS & TECHNIQUES

If you click and hold the mouse while dragging, you create a free-form selection like the Trace tool.

Figure 12. Drag around the area you wish to select to create a free-formed line around the image.

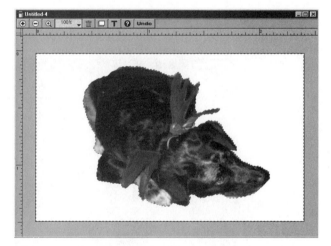

Figure 13. After inverting the selection, pressing the Delete key results in a deleted background of a free-formed shape.

The Trace Tool

The Trace tool creates free-form selections on images. The mouse acts like a pencil, and as you draw a selection is formed by the nuances of the mouse's movements. If you've had limited caffeine and stress, you can create quite a smooth selection around the image.

To create a free-formed selection:

1. Display the Trace tool in the pop-up menu of the Selections palette.

2. Choose the New button to create a new selection.

3. Click and drag a line around the section of the image that you want to select (Figure 12).

To remove the background from a selection:

1. Choose Invert from the Selections palette.

   This will select everything but your original selection.

2. Press the Delete key to remove the background (Figure 13).

   This will fill in the background with white to replace the selection.

   Now that you have made a background white, it will be easy to add a different background or select this object to paste into another document.

Tracing with the Trace Tool

49

The Rectangle Tool

The Rectangle tool creates rectangular selections on the image. By dragging from a corner to the opposite corner, a rectangular selection is created.

To create a rectangular selection:

1. Display the Rectangle tool in the pop-up menu of the Selections palette.

2. Choose the New button to create a new selection.

3. Click and drag out a box around the section of the image that you want to select (Figure 14).

The Oval Tool

The Oval tool creates elliptical selections on the image. By dragging from a corner to the opposite corner, an oval selection is created.

To create an oval selection:

1. Display the Oval tool in the pop-up menu of the Selections palette.

2. Choose the New button to create a new selection.

3. Click and drag out an oval around the section of the image that you want to select (Figure 15).

TIPS & TECHNIQUES

You can draw a perfect square or circle without accessing the Square or Circle tools by holding down the Shift key while dragging with the Rectangle and Oval tools, respectively.

You can draw a rectangular or oval selection from its center if you press and hold the Alt (Option) key before dragging.

Figure 14. Use the Rectangle tool to create a rectangular selection around an image.

Figure 15. Use the Oval tool to create an oval selection around the image.

Using the Rectangle and Oval Tools

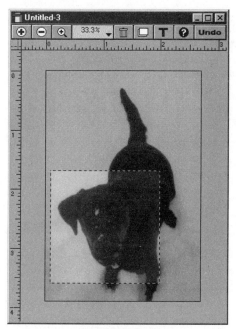

Figure 16. A square selection around the image is created by selecting with the Square tool.

Figure 17. Use the Circle tool to create a circular selection around the image.

The Square Tool

The Square tool creates perfect square selections on the image. By dragging from a corner to the opposite corner, you create a square selection.

To create a square selection:

1. Display the Square tool in the pop-up menu of the Selections palette.

2. Choose the New button to create a new selection.

3. Click and drag a square around the section of the image that you want to select (Figure 16).

The Circle Tool

The Circle tool creates perfect circular selections on the image. By dragging from one "corner" to the opposite "corner," you create a circular selection.

To create a circular selection:

1. Display the Circle tool in the pop-up menu of the Selections palette.

2. Choose the New button to create a new selection.

3. Press and hold the Alt (Option) key and click and drag a circle from the center around the section of the image that you want to select (Figure 17).

TIPS & TECHNIQUES

You can draw a square selection from the center if you press and hold the Alt (Option) key before dragging with the Square tool.

Using the Square and Circle Tools

Color Wand

By clicking on a color that you want to select with the Color Wand, you can select all parts of the image that are the same color. By choosing the Add button, you can add similar colors to that selection. Choosing Reduce will take a color out of the selection.

To create a color selection:

1. Display the Color Wand in the pop-up menu of the Selections palette.

2. Choose the New button to create a new selection.

3. Click on the color you want to select within the image itself (Figure 18).

4. Choose the Add button and click on a new color in the image to add an additional selection (Figure 19).

   This will add the selection with the new color to the original color selection.

Figure 18. Clicking along the top edge of the image with the Color Wand selects a large band of dark blue.

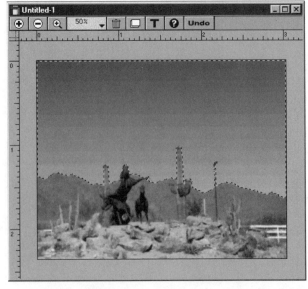

Figure 19. Another color is added to the selection by clicking the Add button, then clicking below the existing selection.

Using the Color Wand

TIPS & TECHNIQUES

Keep in mind that the Color Wand only chooses the *exact* same color. In order to select additional colors, you'll need to click the Add button.

Figure 20. The SmartSelect tool creates lines and points.

Figure 21. After you've finished dragging with the SmartSelect tool, the selection's "marching ants" appear.

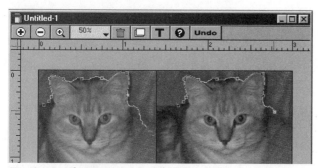

Figure 22. The image on the left shows the current progress of tracing with the SmartSelect tool. The image on the right shows what happens when you backtrack with the tool.

The SmartSelect Tool

The SmartSelect tool is new to PhotoDeluxe 2.0. This ingenious tool creates a selection based on both your tracing and the color edge. The SmartSelect tool will create a selection based on any edge formed by different colors. As you draw, the SmartSelect tool places points down to form the edge of your selection. The benefit to using the SmartSelect tool is that it automatically "snaps" to the edge of a selection, even while you're drawing a loose representation of the intended selection.

This selection is *vector* based, meaning that instead of selecting specific pixels, the selection is a shape which can be modified and adjusted easily.

To create a SmartSelect selection:

1. Display the SmartSelect tool in the pop-up menu of the Selections palette.

2. Choose the New button to create a new selection.

3. Click and start to drag around the edge of where you want to select (Figure 20).

4. After dragging around the entire image, a selection based on both the path you've drawn and the color edges along that path will appear (Figure 21).

TIPS & TECHNIQUES

You can erase if you make a mistake with the SmartSelect tool by backing up the mouse and changing direction (**Figure 22**).

Using the SmartSelect Tool

The Add button

The Add button enables you to add to an existing selection. By keeping this button activated, you can continue to add to any existing selection with whatever Selection tool you choose.

To add to an existing selection:

1. Choose a Selection tool from the Selections palette pop-up menu.

2. Choose the New button and create a new selection (**Figure 23**).

3. Choose the Add button and create a selection (**Figure 24**).

    This adds to the existing selection. If you intersect the existing selection with a new selection, then the selection encompasses both the original selection and the new selection (**Figure 25**).

    You can add as many selections to the original selection as you want. If you added something you didn't want, simply click the Undo button in the document window. In PhotoDeluxe, you can only undo an action one time.

    When making a selection, you don't necessarily have to start with the New button. If you have the Add button selected, you can start with that tool to make your first selection.

Figure 23. A new selection created with the Rectangle tool.

Figure 24. An additional selection has been added to the existing one.

Figure 25. If your second selection touches your first selection, the selections are combined into one selection.

TIPS & TECHNIQUES

You can "Add" a selection to an image that has no current selection. In this case, the Add button works like the New button.

Adding to Existing Selections

Selected area

Figure 26. A New selection created with the SmartSelect tool.

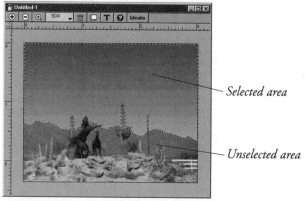

Selected area

Unselected area

Figure 27. The Color Wand was used here to reduce the mountains from the selection.

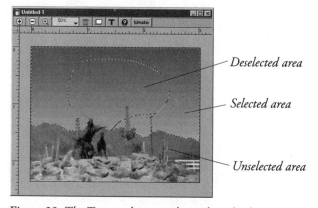

Deselected area

Selected area

Unselected area

Figure 28. The Trace tool was used to reduce this large area from the sky.

The Reduce button

The Reduce button enables you to take away from an existing selection. By keeping this button activated, you can continue to take away from any existing selection with whatever Selection tool you choose.

To reduce an existing selection:

1. Choose a Selection tool from the Selections palette pop-up menu.

2. Choose the New button and create a new selection (Figure 26).

3. Choose the Reduce button and create a selection (Figure 27).

   This reduces the existing selection. If you touch the existing selection with a new reduced selection, then it shrinks to a smaller combination of the two selections (**Figure 28**).

   Keep in mind that you aren't limited to just using the selection tool you started with. You can make a selection with the Color Wand and reduce from that selection using the Trace tool. The Selections window lets you choose any of the tools to mix and match to create the right selection.

Reducing from Existing Selections

The Move button

The Move button moves the whole image, or just a selection. When the image moves, a white fill is left behind where the original position was. The Move button also moves the objects in the Layers palette. See Chapter 9: Combining Photographs for more on Layers.

To move an object on a layer:

1. Create a selection.

2. Choose Edit⇨Copy [Ctrl+C] (Command-C).

   This places a copy of the image on the clipboard, where it can be retrieved later for pasting.

3. Choose Edit⇨Paste [Ctrl+V] (Command-V).

   When an image is pasted, it automatically goes on its own layer.

4. Using the Object Selection tool, scale the image down (Figure 29).

5. Click the Move button and move the image where you want.

6. Choose Edit⇨Paste.

7. Scale this object down.

8. Move the new object where you want (Figure 30).

   You can also move an object on a layer by just clicking on it. Place your cursor in the middle and drag the image to the new location.

   You can also access a layer by clicking on the object you want. That automatically makes the layer with that object on it active.

TIPS & TECHNIQUES

To move an object on a layer, you must first select that layer in the Layers palette.

Figure 29. Scale the pasted image using the Object Selection tool.

Figure 30. Move the objects where you want them to go using the Move button. In this image, we pasted an additional, "evil" copy for placement on the left shoulder.

Moving Selections

USING THE ADVANCED INTERFACE

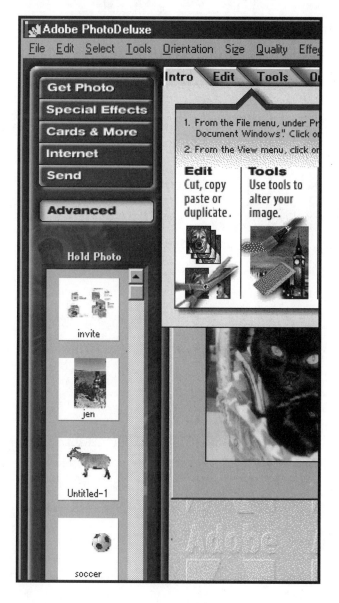

THE Advanced button is the next step for the seasoned user. Instead of being confined to a rigorous set of rules and procedures, you can work at your own pace, doing what you want when you want.

All of PhotoDeluxe's functions are available to you when you click the Advanced button. You can work through the tabs in the program, which will help guide you through specific tasks (but with less handholding than before), or you can just wing it, selecting functions from menus.

How Advanced differs from Guided

Now that you have become comfortable with the Guided Activities, it's time to take the next step. The Guided Activities lead you through specific effects in easy to handle step by steps. The Advanced area lets you create on your own (**Figure 1**). The same tools you access through the Guided Activities are available through the Advanced areas as well. The Advanced area has seven tabbed areas to explore.

The Advanced button lets you use all of PhotoDeluxe's amazing effects without having to follow each step in order. The Advanced button still gives you tabs (and more buttons) for easy manipulation, but you also can explore the array of pull-down menus. The Edit, Tools, Orientation, Size, Quality, and Effects tabs show almost the same things as the pull-down menu (**Figure 2**).

The pull-down menus offer more advanced features. The File, Select, View, Window, and Help menus give you more choices.

The key to working with PhotoDeluxe is making selections. By learning the key to selections, you can affect the whole or a portion of the image. For more information on selections, see Chapter 4: Selection Techniques.

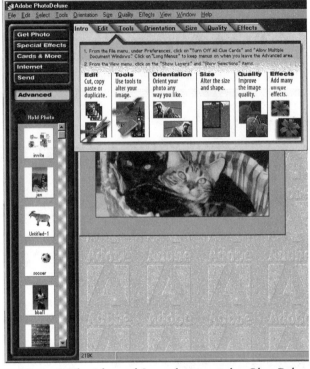

Figure 1. The Advanced Screen lets you explore PhotoDeluxe on your own.

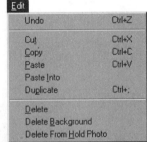

Figure 2. You can access the same tabbed areas with the pull-down menus.

How the Advanced Interface Works

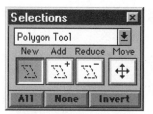

Figure 3. The Selections dialog box.

Figure 4. The Add button adds a selection to the original selection.

Figure 5. Invert selects the opposite of your selection.

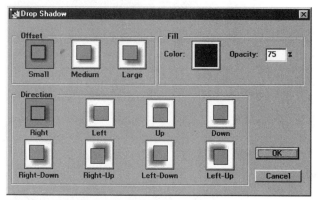

Figure 6. The Drop Shadow dialog box.

Figure 7. The shadow on this gas can is harsh and blunt.

To make a selection in the Advanced areas:

1. Open an image by choosing File⇨Open File or Ctrl+O (Command-O).

   You can also go to the Get Photo button and access your image by clicking on a button.

2. Open the Selections dialog box by choosing View⇨Show Selections (**Figure 3**).

3. Choose the Selection tool you need to use. I chose the Color Wand to select the white background.

4. Click on the white background. If this doesn't get the whole background, then click on the Add button (**Figure 4**).

5. Click the Invert button to select just the object(s) on the white background (**Figure 5**).

6. Click the Effects tab.

7. Click the Drop Shadow button.

   The Drop Shadow dialog box appears (**Figure 6**).

8. Choose the type of drop shadow you wish.

9. Click the OK button (**Figure 7**).

Selecting

TIPS & TECHNIQUES

You can also access each individual selection tool by choosing Select⇨ Selection Tools⇨then choosing the tool you want to use. The only disadvantage to this is that you won't get the Selections window that lets you add, reduce, or select the inverse of your selection.

The shadow on the previous page is a little harsh. The following steps show how to soften it a little, letting it appear more natural.

To soften a shadow:

1. Open the Layers window by choosing View⇨Show Layers (Figure 8).

2. Click the Shadow layer to activate it (Figure 9).

3. Click the Effects tab.

4. Click the Special Effects button.

5. Click the Blur tab.

6. Click the Soften button to activate the Soften dialog box (Figure 10).

7. Soften to your taste, using the preview window on the the left side of the dialog box, then click the OK button to see the effect (Figure 11).

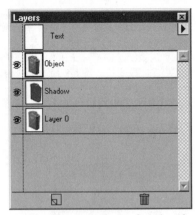

Figure 8. The Layers window is found under the View pull-down menu.

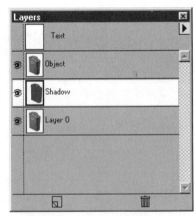

Figure 9. The active layer will appear white and the other layers will be shaded.

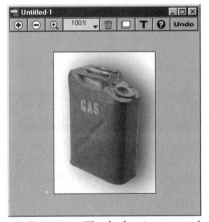

Figure 11. The shadow is now much more natural looking.

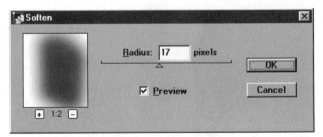

Figure 10. The Soften dialog box lets you see a preview of the soften effect.

Softening Shadows

Figure 12. The black background on this image is a little plain.

Figure 13. The black background is easily selected all at once with the Color Wand.

Figure 14. The final image has a lovely floral background.

Edit tab

The Edit tab enables you to Cut, Copy, Paste, Paste Into, Duplicate, Delete, and Delete Background. The Edit pull-down menu includes Undo and Delete from Hold Photo (see page 74) in addition to the ones found in the Edit tab. One of the coolest functions of the Edit tab is the Paste Into function.

To paste in a picture:

1. Open an image (Figure 12).
2. Open the Selections window by choosing View⮕Show Selections.
3. Click the black background with the Color Wand (Figure 13).
4. Open the picture you want to insert as the background.
5. In the Selections window, choose the All button.
6. In the Advanced area, click the Edit tab.
7. Click the Copy button.
8. Go back to the background image by clicking on the Window menu and dragging down to the name of the background image.
9. In the Edit tab, click the Paste Into button (Figure 14).

The Paste Into function opens the door to many possibilities of photo combinations. You can select a background and totally replace it with a new one. It is also a great way to jazz up a plain background. Any selection you create can be used for the Paste Into function.

Pasting Pictures into Selections

Tools tab

The Tools tab hosts six tools for your editing pleasure. The available tools are: Brush, Color Change, Line, Eraser, Smudge, and Clone. You can access the Text tool if you use the Tools pull-down menu since it isn't available in the Tools tab.

"Cloning" is the process of taking a portion of an image and painting with that portion in another section of the same or a different image.

To clone an image:

1. **Open the image you want to clone (Figure 15).**

2. **Click the Clone button in the Tools tab.**

   The Clone window appears.

3. **Move the Clone crosshairs to the area you want to duplicate (Figure 16).**

4. **Choose a brush size in the Clone window.**

5. **Click on another area of the image to clone the bird's eye (Figure 17).**

   You can repeat this step as often as you'd like, painting again and again with the bird's eye. If you drag (instead of just clicking), you'll clone more of an area.

   Click the Clone button again to pick a new area to clone from.

TIPS & TECHNIQUES

You can move the Clone crosshairs around to clone different parts of your image. You can also clone from one image to another (**Figure 18**). Open both images and size them so you can see both for easier cloning.

Figure 15. The image can be altered by cloning a portion of it.

Figure 16. Select the bird's eye as the area to clone.

Figure 17. You can create some cool patterns using the eye.

Figure 18. Cloning from one image to another lets you add elements between images.

Figure 19. The original image would look great times two.

Figure 20. Hold the Shift key when you move the image to constrain horizontal movement.

Figure 21. The final image with two Santa figurines.

Orientation

The Orientation tab lets you change the orientation of your image. You can Rotate Left, Rotate Right, Flip Horizontal, or Flip Vertical. If you choose to use the Orientation pull-down menu, you'll also find the Free Rotate option.

To copy and flip an image horizontally:

1. Open the image you want to flip (Figure 19).

2. Select the background with the Color Wand.

3. Click the Invert button in the Selections window to select the object.

4. Click the Edit tab.

5. Click the Copy button.

6. Click the Paste button

7. With the arrow in the center of your object, hold the Shift key and move the image to the right (Figure 20).

   The Shift key will restrict the movement of the image to 0, 45, and 90 degrees.

8. Click the Orientation tab.

9. Click the Flip Horizontal button.

   You've created a mirror image of the original (**Figure 21**).

It is really nice to be able to copy and duplicate objects. Unfortunately this doesn't work with money, cars, or homes. Using the copy and flip functions, you can easily create a bunch of flowers from one flower.

Copying and Flipping an Image

Size tab

The Size tab lets you do more than simply change an image's size. The Size options are: Free Resize, Resize, Trim, Distort, Perspective, Canvas Size, and Photo Size. You can change the resolution of the file with the Photo Size button. To add canvas (more white space) to the image, choose Canvas Size.

To change the perspective of an image:

1. Open the image whose perspective you wish to change (Figure 22).

2. Click the Size tab.

3. Click the Perspective button.

4. Drag one of the upper handles inward and one of the lower handles outward (Figure 23).

5. Press the Enter key (on your keyboard) to accept the new perspective (Figure 24).

To resize an image:

1. Open the image to resize.

2. Click the Size tab.

3. Click the Resize button.

4. Drag a corner handle inward to resize the image (Figure 25).

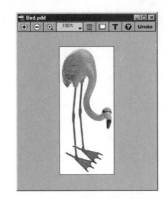

Figure 22. The original image ready for perspective.

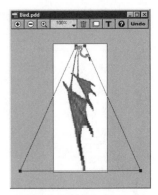

Figure 23. Drag the handles to create your perspective.

Figure 24. The final image "going back" in perspective.

Figure 25. The resized image leaves the canvas size alone and resizes your image only.

TIPS & TECHNIQUES

To equally resize an image, drag a corner handle. To resize disproportionately, drag the center horizontal or center vertical handle. If you change your mind when resizing, press the ESC button.

Figure 26. The parrots can be adjusted to create a whole new look.

Figure 27. The Hue/Saturation dialog box lets you adjust the Hue, Saturation, and Lightness.

Figure 28. The new image has a totally new look.

Quality tab

The Quality tab lets you adjust different attributes of an image. You can adjust the following: Instant Fix, Color Balance, Brightness/Contrast, Hue/Saturation, Sharpen, Remove Dust, and Variations. Even if you buy a photo CD, you'll still need to make adjustments to improve the image quality and clarity. You can make more than one adjustment to an image. By creating a selection, you will only make adjustments to the area within that selection.

To adjust the Hue/Saturation of an image:

1. Open the image you want to adjust (Figure 26).

2. Click the Quality tab.

3. Click the Hue/Saturation button to open the Hue/Saturation window (Figure 27).

4. Adjust the sliders while looking at your image to see the previewed results.

   The Hue/Saturation dialog box lets you change:
   Hue: The color itself (such as red, green, orange, blue, etc.)
   Saturation: How intense the color is. The less saturated an image is, the more it looks gray. The more saturated it is, the more colorful it appears.
   Lightness: The lighter the color, the "brighter" it seems.

5. Click the OK button to accept the new adjustments (Figure 28).

Adjusting Hue and Saturation

Effects tab

The Effects tab adds a special effect to the image. The available effects are: Selection Fill, Gradient Fill, Drop Shadow, Feather, Outline, Color to BW, and Special Effects. The Special Effects button offers five tabbed special effects you can access.

Figure 29. The Special Effects button accesses more special effects.

To create a special effect that defines the edge of your image:

1. Open the image to which you want to add a special effect.

2. Click the Special Effects button to access the special effects choices (Figure 29).

3. Click the Find Edges button (Figure 30).

To create a gradient fill for a background:

1. Open the image you want to use.

2. Select the background using the Color Wand.

3. Click the Advanced button.

4. Click the Effects tab.

5. Click the Gradient Fill button to open the Gradient Fill dialog box (Figure 31).

6. Click the OK button to accept the gradient options (Figure 32).

Figure 30. The Find Edges button outlines an image using the same color pixels as inside the image.

Figure 32. This gradient background gives a baseball photo some interest.

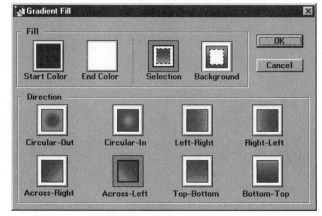

Figure 31. The Gradient Fill window gives you many options for controlling which colors to use and how those colors interact.

Figure 33. *The original apple, waiting for some friends.*

Layers

Layers allow you to work on separate pieces of your image without disturbing other pieces. Any time you copy and paste, PhotoDeluxe automatically creates a new layer. In the Layers window, you can see that text automatically goes on its own layer as well. You can create a new layer in the Layers palette by choosing New Layer from the Layers palette pop-up menu (accessed by clicking and holding on the triangle in the upper right of the palette).

To create a layered image:

1. Open your original image or background image (**Figure 33**).

2. Open another image that you want to add to your background image.

3. Select the image and choose Edit⇨Copy.

4. Go back to the background image and choose Edit⇨Paste.

   This automatically places the new image on its own layer (**Figure 34**).

(continued)

Figure 34. *The orange goes into its own layer.*

Working with Layers

5. Open another image and copy and paste a different object to the background (Figure 35).

6. Choose the layer of the object you want to transform by clicking on that object's layer.

7. Move the objects around to create a fruity scene.

8. Copy and paste more apples, oranges, and bananas to finish off the fruity image (Figure 36).

Any time you paste, the object goes on its own layer. You can access a layer and choose Copy and Paste to paste that same object on a new layer.

Layers let you work with multiple objects on one document. This allows you to easily move, transform, or apply filters to only one object without the hassle of selecting.

Text automatically goes on its own layer. This layer is always on top of the other layers. PhotoDeluxe lets you always edit type which is unlike any other photo manipulation program.

TIPS & TECHNIQUES

To adjust the stacking order of layers, go into the Layers palette and drag one layer above another layer to move that object in front. The top layer in the Layers window is the frontmost object and as you go down, the objects move towards the back. To delete a layer, drag the layer name into the little trash can in the Layers window. You can also add a layer by clicking on the little paper icon at the bottom of the Layers window.

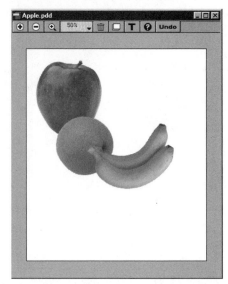

Figure 35. The bananas join the crowd.

Figure 36. The fruity scene is complete.

PRINTING AND EXPORTING

EACH image you create in PhotoDeluxe *can* just stay in the program and rot there, but undoubtedly you'll want to put the image somewhere else, like on a Web page, or on a printed page.

PhotoDeluxe makes printing easy. The Send button in the Activities section—in the upper left of the PhotoDeluxe screen—shows three different send functions. You can send to disk, the Internet, or a printer. You can also access the Send functions from the Edit pull-down menu.

"Exporting" is the process of saving an image for use in another application. For instance, to use a PhotoDeluxe image on the Web, it should be saved as either a JPEG or a GIF file.

The image to the left was scanned into PhotoDeluxe, then the type was added below the image, and finally, the image was printed to an iron-on transfer and placed on a T-shirt.

Send to Disk

The Send to Disk tab lets you create a screensaver, screen wallpaper, save a file, or export to a format different than PhotoDeluxe.

To export a file:

1. **Open the file you want to export.**
2. **Click the Send button in the Activities area of PhotoDeluxe.**
3. **Click the To Disk tab.**
4. **Click the Export button.**
5. **Click the Export tab.**

   There are five different areas to choose from to export a file (**Figure 1**).

6. **Click the Other Export button to display your saving options.**

   The Export Dialog box appears (**Figure 2**).

7. **In the Save As area choose EPS.**
8. **Click the Save button.**

   This will open the EPS Format dialog box (**Figure 3**).

9. **Click the OK button.**

   Now your image is ready to be opened in another application.

Figure 1. The Export tab gives you five exporting options.

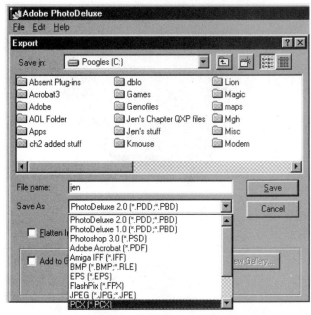

Figure 2. The Other Export button offers you many ways to save a PhotoDeluxe image.

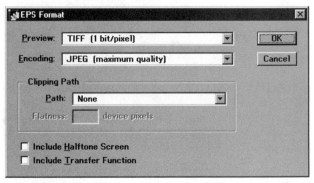

Figure 3. The EPS Format dialog box lets you save a color or black and white file.

TIPS & TECHNIQUES

If you are saving a color image, set the Preview in the EPS Format dialog box to TIFF (8 bits/pixel). The Encoding for the EPS should be set for JPEG (maximum quality).

Exporting

Figure 4. The Printing options for PhotoDeluxe.

Figure 5. The Page Setup dialog box is where you can specify the orientation of your image.

Figure 6. Print Preview shows you what your image will look like before printing.

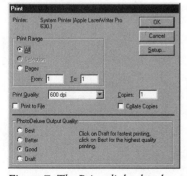

Figure 7. The Print dialog box lets you specify the number of copies you want to print.

Printing is the process of placing the image onto paper (or whatever else works in your printer, such as transparency paper).

To print an image:

1. Open the image you want to print.

2. Click the Send button.

3. Click the To Printer tab to see the Printing options (Figure 4).

4. Click the Page Setup button to activate the Page Setup dialog box (Figure 5).

5. Choose your printer, paper size and source, and image orientation.

    The paper source refers to whether you manually feed a page or use a paper tray. The image orientation is how the image prints on a page. The image can print vertical (or portrait), or it can print horizontal (or landscape).

6. Click the OK button.

7. Click the Print Preview button to view how your image will print on the paper size you specified (Figure 6).

8. Click the OK button.

9. Click the Print button to activate the Print dialog box (Figure 7).

    You can access the page setup from here as well. You can print all pages, only certain pages, set your print quality, the number of copies, and PhotoDeluxe's Output Quality.

10. Choose the number of copies, then click the OK button.

Printing

The Send to Internet function is a preparation area to get your photo ready to use in email, on a web page, in PageMill, or in AT&T WorldNet. You'll actually trim, resize, and reduce your image to save in the proper format for the Internet.

To send to the Internet:

1. Open the file you want to send.

2. Click the Send button in the upper left of the PhotoDeluxe screen.

3. Click the To Internet tab to display your Internet options (Figure 8).

4. Choose PageMill.

5. Click the Trim tab.

6. Click the Trim button and drag a marquee around the area you want to use (Figure 9).

7. Click the OK button to accept this new trimmed image.

8. Click the Size button.

9. Click the Photo Size button to display the Photo Size dialog box and change the size of the photo (Figure 10).

If you are sending a photo over the Internet for viewing on another computer, then you only need to have a resolution of 72 pixels per inch. Computer screens only view images at 72 pixels per inch, so there is no need to have any higher resolution. This also makes the file size smaller and will transfer quicker than a higher resolution file. When creating files for a web page, you need a resolution of 72 pixels per inch.

Figure 8. To view your Internet options, click on the Internet tab.

Figure 9. Drag a marquee around an area to trim it with the Trim button.

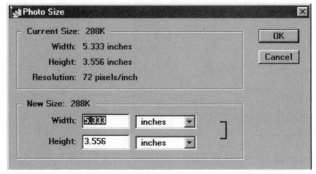

Figure 10. The Photo Size dialog box allows you to change the size of your image.

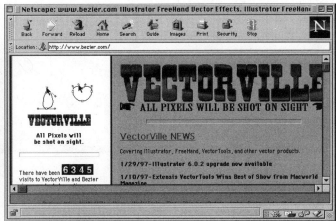

Figure 11a. Drag & Drop is much easier if you can see both applications. The PhotoDeluxe application is shown above.

Figure 11b. The PageMill application is shown above.

10. Click the OK button.

11. Click the Reduce button to reduce the resolution of your image.

12. Click the Drag & Drop tab.

13. Click the Select All button to select the whole image.

14. Hold the mouse button over the image and drag it over your PageMill document (Figure 11). Release the mouse button over the PageMill document.

    Adobe has a great feature with Drag & Drop. With most, if not all, Adobe products, you can drag an image from one application to another.

15. Click the Done button in PhotoDeluxe to finish the activity.

Hold Photo is a box underneath the Activities buttons that stores your photos for easy retrieval.

To send to Hold Photo:

1. **Open the image you want to store in Hold Photo.**

2. **Choose File⇨Send to⇨Hold Photo (Figure 12).**

   The Hold Photo Dialog box appears.

3. **In the Hold Photo dialog box, give your image a name (Figure 13).**

4. **Click the OK button.**

   The photo will show up on the left side of your screen (**Figure 14**).

5. **To access the photo, drag it from the Hold Photo area onto the PhotoDeluxe desktop.**

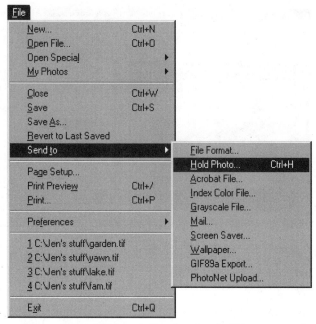

Figure 12. Hold Photo is found under the File menu, under the Send to submenu.

Figure 14. You can quickly access photos from Hold Photo at any time by dragging from the Hold Photo area to your work area.

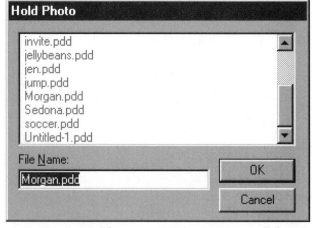

Figure 13. The name you give your image will show up underneath the photo.

Figure 15. You have five export buttons to choose from.

Figure 16. In the Save dialog box, you can change the name of the image.

Figure 17. A PhotoDeluxe file saved in Windows can easily be opened in Acrobat Reader on a Mac.

The Adobe PDF (Portable Document Format) file fomat is a great solution for creating images and documents that need to be viewed on any system. PDF documents can contain images that PhotoDeluxe creates, as well as text and vector-based objects. Adobe Acrobat Reader is free software (download it from www.adobe.com) that allows anyone to view a PDF document. PhotoDeluxe can create PDF files from any document.

To send to an Acrobat file:

1. Open the file you want to make an Acrobat file.

2. Click the Send button.

3. Click the To Disk tab.

4. Click the Export button.

5. Click the Export tab to access the Export options (**Figure 15**).

6. Click the Acrobat File button to bring up the Save dialog box (**Figure 16**).

7. Give the file a name and a location to save it to.

   You'll notice the Save As option is already filled in as Adobe Acrobat [*.PDF].

8. Click the Save button.

   Now this file can easily be opened in Acrobat Reader (**Figure 17**).

Sending to an Acrobat File

TIPS & TECHNIQUES

You can learn all about PDF files and Adobe Acrobat by picking up a copy of Ted's *Acrobat 3 Visual QuickStart Guide for Macintosh and Windows* (Peachpit Press, 1997).

Index Color is a color mode where an image is limited to a specific number of predefined colors. Use Index Color for multimedia and Web page photos.

To send to Index Color file:

1. Open the file you want to use as an Index Color File.

2. Click the Send button.

3. Click the To Disk tab.

4. Click the Export button.

5. Click the Export tab.

6. Click the Index Color button to display the default dialog box for changing an image to index color (Figure 18).

7. Click the Advanced button to open the Indexed Color dialog box (Figure 19).

   You can set the Resolution, Palette, and the Dither of your image in the Indexed Color dialog box.

8. Click the OK button once you have selected your desired settings.

   The Export dialog box appears.

9. Type in a name, file type for your image, and a location for your saved file (Figure 20).

10. Click the Save button to save this image.

    The Palette option in the Indexed Color dialog box lets you choose how your image will be viewed on other systems. If you choose Adaptive, then the image will view at the number of colors on the system that opens the file. If you choose System, then the file will view with the number of colors that the original system had when it was created.

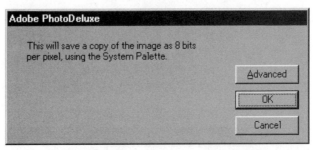

Figure 18. An Index Color File can contain up to 256 colors.

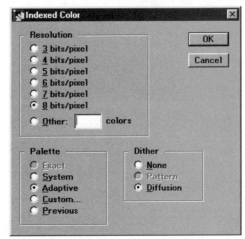

Figure 19. The Advanced button gives you more options for saving.

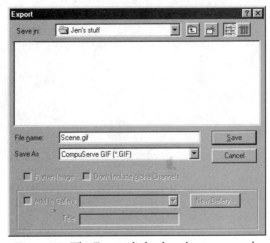

Figure 20. The Export dialog box that appears when you're exporting the image as a GIF file.

Figure 21. The Export dialog box is where you can save the name, location, and file type.

Grayscale images

A grayscale image is a much smaller file size than a color image. There is no reason to save a file in color if you are only ever using it as a grayscale image.

Grayscale images are great to use for painting in with color. You need to change the file to RGB first, but you can create some amazing old-time painted photos. By using any photo you have now, you can change it to grayscale, then back to RGB to add color in again. To soften the edges between grayscale and color, use a feather on your selection.

To send to a Grayscale file:

1. Open the file you want to make grayscale.

2. Click the Send button.

3. Click the To Disk tab.

4. Click the Export button.

5. Click the Export tab.

6. Click the Grayscale button.

   The Export dialog box appears (**Figure 21**).

7. Enter the name of the file, the type of file you want to save as, and the location of the file.

8. Click the Save button.

   Your original image will still be in color, but the new saved image will be in grayscale.

Sending to a Grayscale File

Sending files through email has become easy to do. The following steps take you through the process of exporting an image so that it can be attached to email and read by anyone.

To send a file through email:

1. Open the file you want to prepare for sending by email.

2. Click the Send button.

3. Click the To Internet tab.

4. Click the Email button (Figure 22).

5. Click the Size tab.

6. Click the Photo Size button to activate the Photo Size dialog box (Figure 23).

7. Click the Reduce tab.

8. Click the Reduce Resolution button to change the resolution to 72 dpi.

9. Click the Mail tab (Figure 24).

10. Click the Mail button if you use Windows Messaging, or the JPEG format if you use another mail program.

    I chose the JPEG format since I use another mailing program.

11. In the Export dialog box, give the file a name and a location (Figure 25).

12. Click the Save button.

13. Click the Done button to end the activity.

    People use many different types of email programs. We find it best to save one file per email note and not to compress the file. Compression programs aren't always compatible on other systems. You also have to keep in mind if you are sending it to a Mac or Windows system.

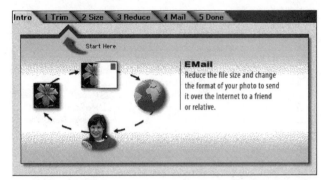

Figure 22. To prepare a file for email, click the Email button.

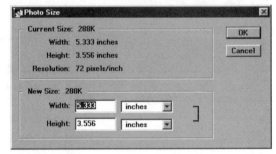

Figure 23. The Photo Size dialog box lets you resize your photo.

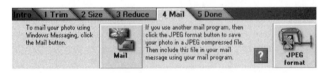

Figure 24. The Mail tab shows you two mailing options, Windows Messaging or a JPEG format.

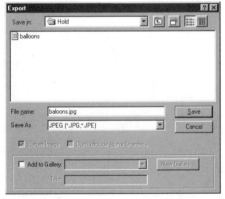

Figure 25. In the Export dialog box, give your file a name and a save location.

Sending to Email

Figure 26. Choose any file to make wallpaper.

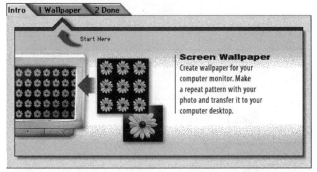

Figure 27. The Intro tab shows how Wallpaper works.

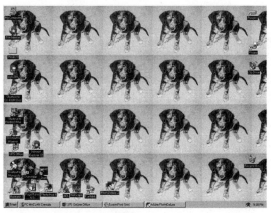

Figure 28. The new wallpaper can be any critter you wish.

Wallpaper

With Wallpaper, you can use any picture you might have. You may want to save the file you are making into wallpaper somewhere on your hard drive. If you make another image into wallpaper, the first image is replaced. Windows only lets you have one PhotoDeluxe wallpaper file at a time. When you save each photo, then you can easily open up the file and make it into wallpaper again.

You can have the whole image take up your screen, or tile the image so it repeats. We recommend you choose a wallpaper you can live with. If the wallpaper is complex, it may get annoying to see when you are having a long, bad day. We like to use happy, simplistic images that are easy on the eyes.

To send a file to use as wallpaper:

1. Open the file you want to make Wallpaper (Figure 26).
2. Click the Send button.
3. Click the Screen/Wallpaper button.
4. Click the Wallpaper tab.
5. Click the Wallpaper button (Figure 27).
6. Go to your desktop to see the results (Figure 28).

Sending to Wallpaper

GIF89a

The GIF89a file format is one of the most popular formats for web page images and onscreen displays. Each GIF89a image contains a specific number of colors, reducing file size dramatically. In addition, GIF89a files can contain transparency (so you can see areas behind the image that don't have to be outside the rectangular boundaries of the image) and can be used for image maps (areas within an image that point to different URLs).

To export a GIF89a file:

1. Open the file you want to export.

2. Click the Send button.

3. Click the To Disk tab.

4. Click the Export tab.

5. Click the GIF Format button to open the GIF89a Export Options (Figure 29).

6. Click the Advanced button to see more options (Figure 30).

7. Choose your palette from the available list.

   We prefer Adaptive. If you choose System, the file will only have the number of colors your system has. If you choose Adaptive, the file will adapt to any system colors.

8. Click the OK button.

   The Export dialog box will appear.

9. Give the file a name and a location to save it.

10. Click the Save button.

    A window will come up letting you know the file has been saved as GIF89a format (**Figure 31**).

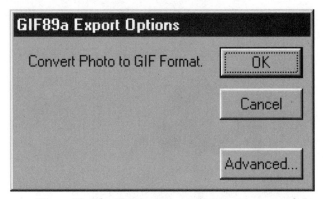

Figure 29. The GIF89a Export Options gives you a choice between easy or advanced.

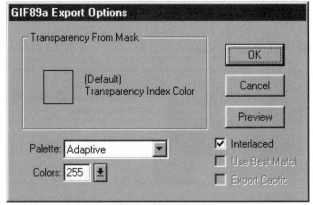

Figure 30. The Advanced button takes you to another dialog box where you can choose more options.

Figure 31. It's comforting to know that the file has been saved.

Figure 32. The T-Shirt file is ready for printing.

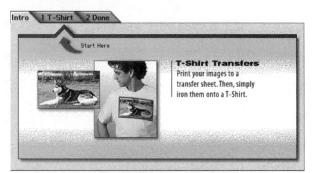

Figure 33. The Intro explains what will happen.

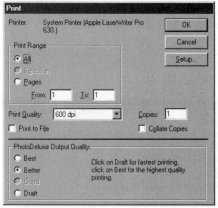

Figure 34. The Print dialog box is where you'll need to specify manual feed to put in your transfer paper.

Any image you create in PhotoDeluxe can be made into a T-Shirt transfer. That means any cool photos you take and scan in to PhotoDeluxe can be made into a T-Shirt.

To print a T-Shirt transfer:

1. Open the file you want to use for a T-Shirt transfer (Figure 32).

2. Click the Send button.

3. Click the To Printer tab.

4. Click the Print T-Shirt button and read the Intro (Figure 33).

5. Click the T-Shirt tab.

6. Click the T-Shirt button to open the Print dialog box (Figure 34).

7. Click the Done button to end the activity.

You'll need to insert a transfer sheet in your printer, and the image will print out as a mirror image. The image will look fine when ironed on a T-Shirt.

Now that you can create a T-Shirt transfer, there is nothing to stop you from starting your own T-Shirt shop. You can also create your own Christmas gifts with these transfers. If you print a color print of the image, and print a transfer, your gift recipients will see exactly how the image will look.

Printing to a T-Shirt Transfer

Using PhotoDeluxe images with other applications

Now that you have seen many of the exporting functions of PhotoDeluxe, you'll find you can save any file to open in another application.

To save and open a PhotoDeluxe file in another application:

1. Open the file you want to save (Figure 35).

2. Click the Send button.

3. Click the To Disk tab.

4. Click the Export button.

5. Click the Export tab.

6. Click the Other Export button.

7. Give the file a name, file type, and a location so you can find it easily (Figure 36).

   Choose IBM PC or Macintosh format options if you're saving the image in TIFF format (Figure 37).

9. Click the OK button.

   We talk about saving as a TIFF image because it is the most versatile file type to use in other programs. You can export many different file types: PhotoDeluxe 2.0, PhotoDeluxe 1.0, Photoshop 3.0, Adobe Acrobat, Amiga IFF, BMP, EPS, FlashPix, JPEG, PCX, PICT File, PNG, Targa, and TIFF.

   Before exporting a file, find out what program you'll be opening it in. After choosing the program, check to see which file type is the best to use in that particular program.

Figure 35. The original file is ready for export.

Figure 36. Give the file a name and a location so you can find it later.

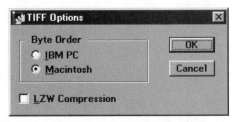

Figure 37. Choose the format type depending on whether the file is going to a PC or a Mac.

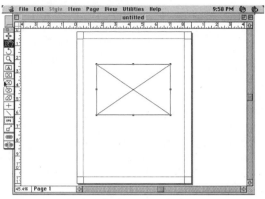

Figure 38. The picture box is ready for a picture.

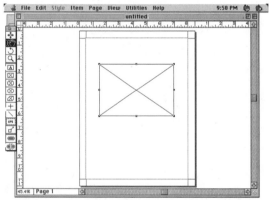

Figure 39. You can resize the image in QuarkXPress (or any other page layout program) easily.

Figure 40. The layout is complete.

10. **Open another application.**

    I chose QuarkXPress on the Macintosh.

11. **Draw a picture box in QuarkXPress using the Rectangular Picture Box Creation tool (Figure 38).**

12. **Choose File⇨Get Picture.**

13. **Double-click on the saved file from PhotoDeluxe.**

14. **Resize the image if needed (Figure 39).**

15. **Finish the layout (Figure 40).**

    QuarkXPress or Adobe PageMaker favor TIFF or EPS files. These file types will print the best quality and view better than other file types.

    Adobe Illustrator and Adobe Photoshop can open many different formats as well. EPS and TIFF images work best in these programs as well.

    If you are exporting a file that will stay on a Windows 95 system, be sure to note any options that save to IBM PC. If you save a file as Macintosh, it won't open on a Windows system. If you save an IBM PC file, you *can* open that file on a Macintosh system.

Using Images with Other Programs

Color vs. Black and White

You can print your image in color or black and white. When you print, choose the appropriate printer, either your black and white printer or your color printer. If the file is in color, it will print in color on the color printer, and as black and white on the black and white printer. You can also save the file as a grayscale image if you know it will always stay black and white. Many graphics people find it easier to take their image into another program (such as PageMaker or QuarkXPress) to finish it off with layout, type, and printing.

Separations

Many artists want all four colors printed out as separations so they can get their work printed on a commercial printing press. PhotoDeluxe doesn't have a separations option, but you can save the file and open it in another application that does print separations. When you save the file as an EPS or TIFF, place it in PageMaker, QuarkXPress, Illustrator, or Photoshop to print your separations.

WEB PAGES AND EMAIL

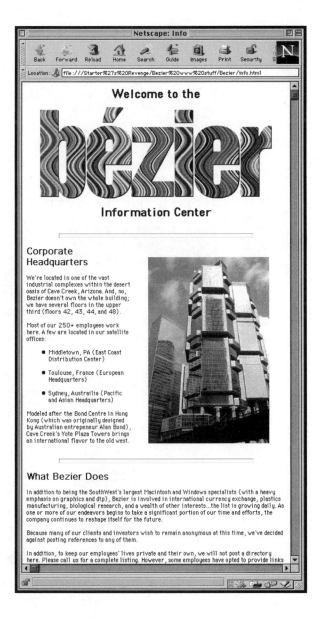

THE world has become linked through widescale use of the Internet. PhotoDeluxe provides you with the capabilities to add images to Web pages, grab images from Web pages, and send images via email.

PhotoDeluxe is the perfect program for creating images for your Web page. With the integration of Adobe's products, creating a Web page is easier than ever. Even images started in a vector program can be softened in PhotoDeluxe and prepared for Web pages. With drag and drop capabilities between Adobe products, creation of Web pages is even easier.

To download an image from the Web:

1. Click the Internet button.

2. Click the Internet tab.

3. Click the Adobe button to access the Adobe Web page (Figure 1).

   This will bring up the Connect To dialog box asking for your password to log on.

   On some systems, you may have to connect to the Internet by a different method. Please see your ISP's (Internet Service Provider) instructions on connection.

4. **Enter a new Web address: http://www.bezier.com.**

   This will bring up a Web page where you can access art files (**Figure 2**).

Figure 1. Open the Adobe Web page to log on.

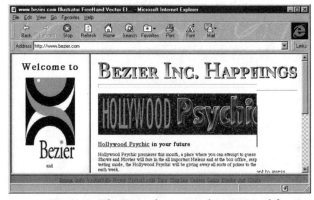

Figure 2. The Bezier home page has some cool features.

TIPS & TECHNIQUES

When moving around in Web pages, look for underlined type or type that is a different color. These indicators will take you another part of the Web site. Some Web sites have actual buttons that you can click on to access another section.

Most Internet providers offer a search screen. That way if you don't know an internet address, you can search topics to find the one you want.

The Internet is a great place to do research, find entertainment, and send mail. There are so many different Web sites to visit. Visit our Website at www.bezier.com.

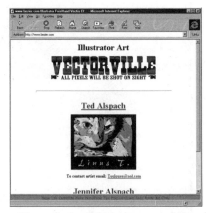

Figure 3. By clicking on an underlined word, you go to that link.

Downloading Web Images

Figure 4. A left mouse click accesses a menu, which lets you save a file.

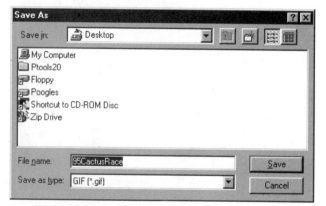

Figure 5. In the Save As dialog box, save the file to your drive for use in PhotoDeluxe.

Figure 6. The image opens up in PhotoDeluxe and is ready to use.

5. Click on the word Art at the bottom of the Bezier Web page (Figure 3).

6. Click on the name "Ted Alspach" to see more of his art.

7. Click on the art you want to download to PhotoDeluxe (Figure 4).

8. Choose the Save Picture As option to open the Save As dialog box (Figure 5).

9. Go back to PhotoDeluxe and open the file (Figure 6).

If you are trying to sell any product, the Web is a great place to do it. We use the Internet to order flowers, advertise our artistic talents, and sell consulting services.

The only catch to the Internet is that it is difficult to get away from it. Once you start surfing the net, there is no turning back. You'll find that you spend more and more time on your computer than you ever thought you would.

Downloading Web Images

Buttons for Web pages

One of the many uses of PhotoDeluxe is to create unique buttons for your Web page. You can use an existing image to create a button, or you can start with a blank page and create your own from scratch.

To create a basic button:

1. Choose File⇨New to open a new document.

   The New dialog box appears. You can also press Ctrl+N (Command-N) to open a new document.

2. Give the file a name, size, and resolution (Figure 7).

3. Click the OK button.

4. Click the Advanced button.

   This will show you all of the available pull-down menus.

5. Choose View⇨Show Selections to access the Selections dialog box.

6. Use the Oval selection tool and hold the Shift key while you drag to create a circle (Figure 8).

   When you hold the Shift key, the Oval tool draws a perfect circular selection. Holding the Alt key (Option) will draw an oval from the center.

7. Click the Effects tab.

8. Click the Gradient Fill button to access the Gradient Fill window (Figure 9).

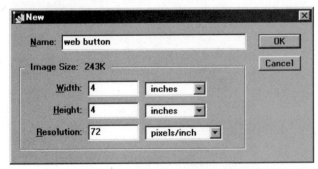

Figure 7. The New dialog box lets you choose the size and resolution of your new document.

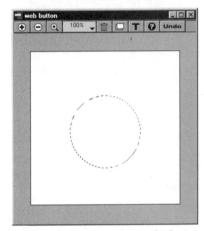

Figure 8. Using the Oval selection tool is one way to create a button.

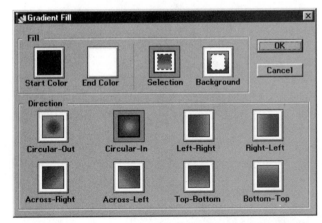

Figure 9. The Gradient Fill dialog box has a Circular-Out choice that works great for a 3D button.

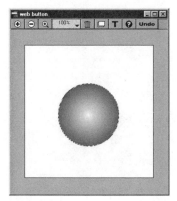

Figure 10. The gradient goes from blue to black in a radial pattern.

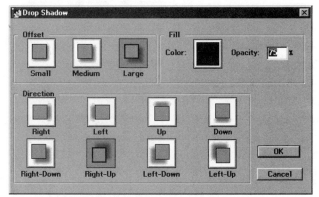

Figure 11. The Drop Shadow dialog box.

9. Choose your start and end color and the direction of the gradient.

10. Click the OK button.

    The object will be filled with the gradient (**Figure 10**).

11. Click the Drop Shadow button to create a shadow for your new button.

    This opens the Drop Shadow dialog box (**Figure 11**).

12. Choose the type of shadow you want, then click the OK button (**Figure 12**).

13. Choose View⇨Show Layers.

14. Click on the Shadow layer to activate that layer.

15. Click the Special Effects button.

16. Click the Blur tab.

17. Click the Soften button to open the Soften dialog box.

18. Click the OK button when you see the desired softness on your shadow (**Figure 13**).

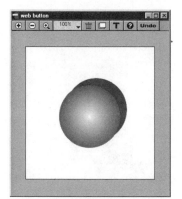

Figure 12. The shadow appears behind the button.

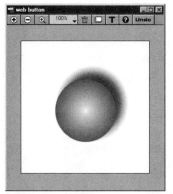

Figure 13. The soft shadow gives the illusion of 3D.

Creating Buttons

89

To create a textured button:

1. Open an image that has a textured look (Figure 14).

2. Click the Advanced button.

3. Choose the Circle tool from the Selections dialog box.

4. Draw a circle in the center of your textured image (Figure 15).

5. Choose Invert in the Selections dialog box.

6. Click the Quality tab.

7. Click the Brightness/Contrast button.

   The Brightness/Contrast dialog box appears.

8. Increase the Brightness to 50 and decrease the Contrast to -50.

9. Click the OK button to see the effect (Figure 16).

   Web buttons are a clear indicator of where to select something on your Web page. You can create a Web button out of anything. Some of the more creative buttons we've seen are eyeball buttons, finger buttons, and manhole cover buttons. You can make any image into a Web button.

Figure 14. A textured image makes a great button for the Web.

Figure 15. The Circle tool creates a perfect circle without having to hold the Shift key.

Figure 16. Altering the background will make the button stand out.

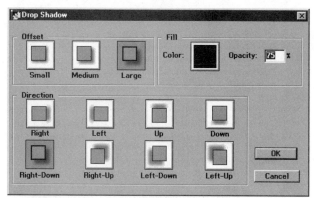

Figure 17. The Drop Shadow dialog box opens when you click the Drop Shadow button.

Figure 18. The shadow is a little harsh.

Figure 19. The Soften effect creates a nice shadow for the textured button.

10. Click the Invert button in the Selections dialog box.

11. Click the Effects tab.

12. Click the Drop Shadow button to open the Drop Shadow dialog box (Figure 17).

13. After entering the Offset, Fill, and Direction, click the OK button (Figure 18).

14. In the Layers window, click on the Shadow layer to activate that layer.

15. Click the Special Effects button.

16. Click the Blur tab.

17. Click the Soften button.

18. After dragging out a nice blur, click the OK button to see the final effect (Figure 19).

    Shadows make your button appear more three dimensional. You can make a shadow on any button and you aren't limited to making a black shadow. The shadow can be any color you want.

Creating Textured Buttons

To incorporate a button you've created into a Web page, you'll need to export it in a format that Web page creation software (such as Adobe PageMill) can use.

Getting your button ready for PageMill:

1. Open the button image you wish to use (Figure 20).

2. Click the Send button.

3. Click the To Disk tab.

4. Click the Export button.

5. Click the Export tab.

6. Click the GIF Format button.

   The GIF89A Export Options dialog box appears.

7. Click the Advanced button to access more options (Figure 21).

8. Give the button a name and location so you can access it in PageMill.

Figure 20. The textured button is ready for placing into a PageMill document.

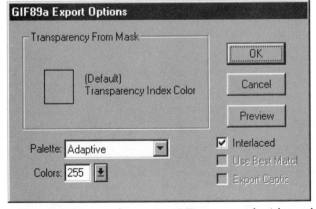

Figure 21. You can change your GIF options in the Advanced portion of the GIF89a Export Options dialog box.

Preparing Buttons for Web Pages

Figure 22. Vector-based art is easily brought into PhotoDeluxe.

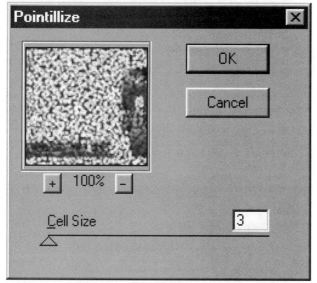

Figure 23. The Pointillize dialog box lets you see a small preview of your effect.

Vector artwork

Vector files are images that consist of filled and stroked outlines.

Any image you create in Illustrator can be brought into PhotoDeluxe for further enhancments. Illustrator is great for creating a basic vector-based illustration, but PhotoDeluxe is the program you'll use to add texture, shadow and light effects.

Many people will add realism to their vector-based clip art images in PhotoDeluxe. When you make a selection, you can apply special effects to portions of your vector-based images.

To open a vector file and enhance the images with PhotoDeluxe:

1. Open the vector file in PhotoDeluxe (Figure 22).
2. Click the Advanced button.
3. Click the Effects tab.
4. Click the Special Effects button.
5. Click the Pointillize button to open the Pointillize dialog box (Figure 23).
6. Choose a small cell size for a more subtle effect.
7. Click the OK button to see the results (Figure 24).

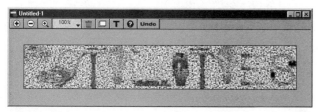

Figure 24. The final vector art has a new look with Pointillize.

Opening a Vector File in PhotoDeluxe

Email and photos

Now that you're getting the hang of getting files ready, let's say you want to send this great photo to a friend using your email program. That shouldn't be a problem. Scan your photo right into PhotoDeluxe and make any changes you want. The nice thing about PhotoDeluxe is that you can enhance the original photo to make yourself look better.

You can send files with any email software, but the following steps are specifically for sending a file with Claris Emailer. If you'll be using another email package (such as Eudora or Netscape Communicator), the steps will be the same until step 14, at which point they may differ slightly.

Sending a file with Claris Emailer:

1. Scan in the photo you want to send (Figure 25).

2. Click the Send button.

3. Click the To Internet tab.

4. Click the Email button.

5. If you need to trim the photo, click the Trim button.

6. Click the Size button to resize your photo.

7. Click the Resize button to enter the new size using the Photo Size dialog box (Figure 26).

8. Click the OK button.

9. Click the Reduce button to change the resolution.

Figure 25. Any photo you have in PhotoDeluxe can be sent all around the world.

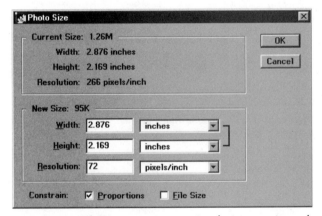

Figure 26. You may want to resize the image so it can be easily opened.

Figure 27. You can send a note to a friend or relative, along with a photo.

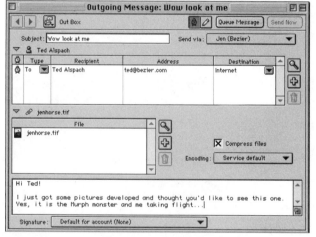

Figure 28. The paperclip will show your file's name.

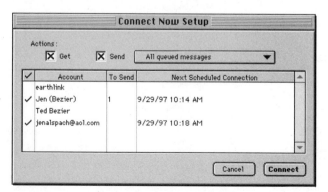

Figure 29. After you're connected to the Internet, send the email. The file will be sent along with it automatically.

10. Click the Reduce Resolution button to automatically change the resolution to 72 dpi.

11. Click the Mail tab.

12. Click the JPEG format button for your mailing program.

13. Enter a name for the file and click the OK button to save it.

14. Open Claris Emailer.

15. From the Mail pull-down menu choose New Mail.

16. Type in your message (Figure 27).

17. Open the saved photo in another window.

18. Drag and drop the image onto the message (Figure 28).

    A paperclip will appear in the message dialog box to indicate that an image is attached to the outgoing message.

19. Click the Send Now button to send your note with photo immediately or use the Connect Now Setup dialog box to send multiple messages at once (Figure 29).

If you're sending via Netscape Navigator/Communicator:

After you type your message using the Netscape software, click the Attach button, select the image file you want to send, click OK, and then send your mail.

TOUCHING UP IMAGES

COLORS in PhotoDeluxe are a tricky business. In a perfect world, colors would always look right when they were brought into your computer, regardless of whether they were scanned, from a CD-ROM, or a Web page.

Unfortunately, the truth isn't nearly so bright (or contrasty). Instead, pictures often come in to PhotoDeluxe needing some heavy duty touch-up work to make them look better.

Fixing red-eye or a glassy-looking eye

Red-eye or a glassy-looking eye is one of the most common photograph problems. Looking directly at the flash results in the dark part of the eye turning red or glassy. This can be fixed in PhotoDeluxe with just the click of a button.

To fix a red-eye or glassy-eyed photo:

1. Open the offending photo (Figure 1).

2. Click the Get Photo button.

3. Click the Touch Up tab.

4. Click the Remove Red Eye buttton.

5. Click the Select tab.

6. Click the Select Rectangle button.

7. Drag a rectangle around the eyes (Figure 2).

8. Click the Remove tab.

9. Click the Remove Red Eye button.

10. Click the Done tab to finish the activity (Figure 3).

    Remove Red Eye works well with the glassy-looking eye. Anytime you have eyes in which the iris is cloudy, try using Remove Red Eye first to fix it. If Remove Red Eye isn't enough, then try using Brightness/Contrast to clear up the image more.

Figure 1. Animal pictures almost always come out with a glassy-looking pair of eyes.

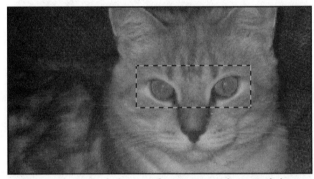

Figure 2. You only have to draw a rectangle around the eyes.

Figure 3. Toulouse looks so much better and clearer after using Remove Red Eye.

Figure 4. The original photo shows a blue-eyed boy.

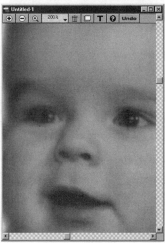

Figure 5. Zoom in so you can select more easily.

Figure 6. The Color Picker dialog box lets you pick a foreground and background color.

To change the color of eyes:

1. Open the photo you want to change (Figure 4).
2. Click the Get Photo button.
3. Click the Touch Up tab.
4. Click the Color Eye button.
5. Click the Zoom tab.
6. Click the Zoom tool and drag a marquee around the eyes to zoom in.
    The image will zoom to the area you surrounded (**Figure 5**).
7. Click the Select tab.
8. Click the Color Wand button.
9. Click on the colored part of the eyes until all of the color is selected.
10. Click the Color tab.
11. Click the Color button to pick a color from the Color Picker dialog box (Figure 6).
12. Click the Paint tab.
13. Touch up any areas that need it.
14. Click the Done tab to see the

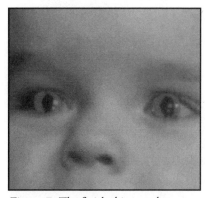

Figure 7. The finished image shows a bright, reptilian-looking green-eyed boy (as best it can, the image being in black and white here). Now if there was only a filter to shrink that forehead a bit...

Instant Fix is a great way to take the guesswork out of fixing your images. Instant Fix will try to fix your image by checking the light and dark as well as the sharpness of the image.

To instantly fix an image:

1. Open the photo that needs to be fixed (Figure 8).

2. Click the Get Photo button.

3. Click the Touch Up tab.

4. Click the Instant Fix button to see your results (Figure 9).

   As a general rule, we always try Instant Fix on every photo. Most people think that when they buy a stock CD with photos that the photos are perfect in quality. The fact is that everyone's taste differs in terms of quality. What we think looks good, you may think needs more adjustment.

Figure 8. The original image is dark and cloudy.

Figure 9. Instant Fix totally fixes the bad photo.

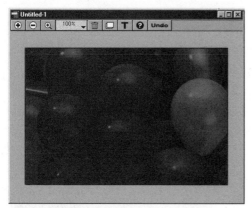

Figure 10. The original color a little dark; maybe it needs some tweaking.

Figure 11. The Variations dialog box shows you a preview of the changes you make.

Figure 12. The final image looks much better.

To adjust the color balance of an image:

1. Open the photo that needs to be fixed (Figure 10).

2. Click the Get Photo button.

3. Click the Touch Up tab.

4. Click the Fix Color button.

5. Click the Variations tab.

6. Click the Variations button to bring up the Variations dialog box (Figure 11).

7. Adjust the Variations and click the OK button.

8. Click the Done tab to finish the color adjustment (Figure 12).

   Variations are easy to use when you look at the dialog box as a wheel. Whatever color is opposite will balance out the overbearing color. If you click once on each color all around, you'll end up with no change at all, since each color can be cancelled by the color opposite of it.

Color Balance Adjustment

To adjust the Brightness/Contrast:

1. Open the dull image (Figure 13).

2. Click the Advanced button.

3. Click the Quality tab.

4. Click the Brightness/Contrast button to activate the Brightness/Contrast dialog box (Figure 14).

5. Adjust the sliders while looking at your image.

6. Click the OK button to finish the adjustment (Figure 15).

Usually increasing the contrast in an image fixes the quality of the image. If the image is too dark, you'll need to increase the brightness and the contrast as well. If you are looking to put text over your image and want to lighten the area, you can make a selection and brighten that particular selection. After brightening that section, black text will show up nicely on top.

Figure 13. The original image is dull and unclear.

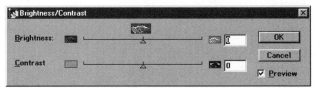

Figure 14. The Brightness/Contrast dialog box lets you preview your changes.

Figure 15. The final image looks much clearer.

Figure 16. The original image is really blurry.

Figure 17. The final image looks much crisper.

As it happens, cameras that were out 30 years ago weren't the best in reproducing a image. Many photos that lack clarity and tend to be blurry can be fixed by using Sharpen. The cameras back then were probably the best at that time, but not now. Fortunately with PhotoDeluxe, you can take any image that is blurry, dark or lacks contrast and scan into PhotoDeluxe. Once in PhotoDeluxe, you can make those images almost like new again.

To sharpen a blurry photo:

1. Open the blurry photo (Figure 16).
2. Click the Advanced button.
3. Click the Quality tab.
4. Click the Sharpen button.

   The image gets clearer (Figure 17).

   You may have to click the Sharpen button several times to achieve the desired effect.

If you've ever scanned in a high school photo from a yearbook, you may have noticed the tiny dots that make up the faces. If you apply a slight blur, those dots will disappear. Blur also works great to soften a background which makes your foreground stand out better.

To blur an image that is too harsh:

1. Open the harsh image (Figure 18).

2. Click the Advanced button.

3. Click the Effects tab.

4. Click the Special Effects button.

5. Click the Blur tab.

6. Click the Soften button to access the Soften dialog box.

7. As you drag the slider, watch the photo to see the softening results.

8. Click the OK button to complete the change (Figure 19).

Figure 18. The original image is very harsh looking.

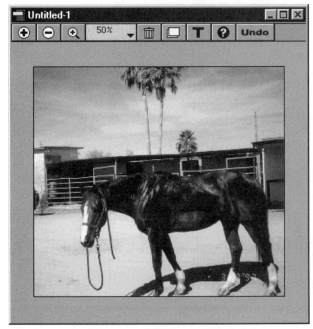

Figure 19. The final image looks much softer.

Figure 20. The original image needs a more interesting background.

Figure 21. The initial click only selects some of the sky.

Noise works great to add some texture to a background. You also might want to consider using more than one effect to change a background. Like for instance adding noise to a background, then adding a swirled effect. There is no limit to how many effects you can apply to a selection.

To add noise to give a background texture:

1. Open the original image (Figure 20).
2. Click the Advanced button.
3. View the Selections window by choosing View⇨Show Selections.
4. Choose the Color Wand.
5. Click on the blue sky background (Figure 21).
6. Click the Add button to add to that selection.

(Continued)

Adding Noise

7. Keep clicking on all of the sky to select the whole background (Figure 22).

8. Click the Effects tab.

9. Click the Special Effects button.

10. Click the Blur tab.

11. Click the Noise button to access the Noise dialog box (Figure 23).

12. Click the Minus button to zoom out in the Noise dialog box so you can see the background.

13. Adjust the slider and click the OK button to see your results (Figure 24).

Figure 22. The Add button lets you select the rest of the sky.

Figure 24. The final image has a more exciting background.

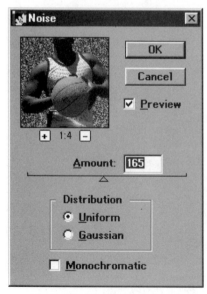

Figure 23. The Noise dialog box lets you see a preview of your added noise.

Figure 25. The Aloha deck of a cruise ship, with its passengers oblivious to the terror that awaits them in Figure 27.

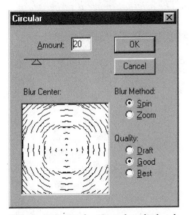

Figure 26. In the Circular dialog box you can choose Spin or Zoom.

Figure 27. The cruise ship is sucked into the netherworld, where the passengers must watch Love Boat reruns for eternity.

To create a circular effect:

1. Open the file you want to add the effect to (Figure 25).

2. Click the Advanced button.

3. Click the Effects tab.

4. Click the Special Effects button.

5. Click the Blur tab.

6. Click the Circular button to access the Circular dialog box (Figure 26).

7. Choose a Spin or Zoom method, the quality, and the amount.

8. Click the OK button to see the effect (Figure 27).

Creating a Circular Effect

TIPS & TECHNIQUES

Using the Circular effect is another way to create a textured background. You can use the Selection tools to apply the effect to only a portion of your image. You can also try this with a colored image to which you already added noise for an even more dramatic effect.

To make your image fight the wind:

1. Open the image to which you want to add a wind effect (Figure 28).

2. View the Selections dialog box by choosing View⇨Show Selections.

3. Using the Color Wand, select the white background (Figure 29).

4. Click the Advanced button.

5. Click the Effects tab.

6. Click the Selection Fill button to activate the Selection Fill dialog box (Figure 30).

PhotoDeluxe offers more than a plain fill for your selection. Try experimenting with some of the pattern fills. You can always apply an effect on top of the pattern fill.

PhotoDeluxe lets you change almost anything in your image. You can place yourself anywhere on or off of this earth with a little time and effort in learning all of the aspects of PhotoDeluxe.

Figure 28. The original image is rather plain.

Figure 29. The Color Wand works great with a solid background.

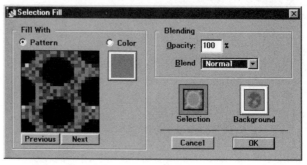

Figure 30. You can fill a selection with a color or a pattern.

Adding a Wind Effect

Figure 31. The new fill pattern adds an exciting background.

7. Choose a pattern with which to fill the selection.

8. Click the OK button to accept that fill (Figure 31).

9. With that same selection still active, click the Special Effects button.

10. Click the Wind button to activate the Wind dialog box (Figure 32).

11. Choose a method and a direction for the wind, then click the OK button to see the effect (Figure 33).

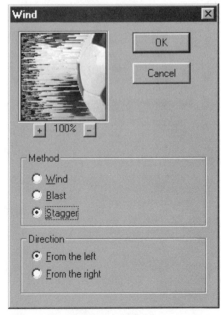

Figure 32. The Wind dialog box gives you three wind choices.

Figure 33. The final image has much more punch.

Adding Wind

The Dust and Scratches effect not only works on scratched or damaged images. It also works great on shiny bright spots on people's bald heads, or those same spots on bulbous noses. To soften a bright shiny head or nose, you need to select around the shiny spot, then apply the Dust and Scratches effect.

To remove dust or scratches from an image:

1. Open the offending image (Figure 34).

2. Click the Advanced button.

3. Click the Quality tab.

4. Click the Remove Dust button to open the Dust & Scratches dialog box (Figure 35).

5. Click the OK button to accept the adjustment (Figure 36).

Figure 34. The original image has a few scratches across it.

Figure 35. A small number in radius is enough to correct the scratches in the Dust & Scratches dialog box.

Figure 36. The final image is perfect.

Figure 37. The original photo is light, blurry, and lacks contrast.

Figure 38. The Instant Fix button gets you started on the right track.

Figure 39. The Sharpen button crisps up the blurry image.

Using multiple effects to fix an image:

1. Open a photo that is too light and blurry (Figure 37).

2. Click the Advanced button.

3. Click the Quality tab.

4. Click the Instant Fix button to begin the fixing process (Figure 38).

5. Click the Sharpen button a few times to crisp up the image (Figure 39).

6. Click the Brightness/Contrast button to open the Brightness/Contrast dialog box.

7. Adjust the sliders to fix the image.

8. Click the OK button to finish the image (Figure 40).

Figure 40. The final image is much brighter.

Using combined effects on an image:

1. Open the first image to be fixed (Figure 41).

2. Click the Advanced button.

3. Click the Quality tab.

4. Click the Sharpen button until the image is crisp (Figure 42).

5. Open the Selections dialog box by choosing View⇨Show Selections.

6. Using the Color Wand, select the white background.

7. Click the Invert button in the Selections dialog box so only the goat is selected.

8. Click the Edit tab.

9. Click the Copy button.

10. Open a background image that needs fixing (Figure 43).

    When you paste the same image multiple times, try to alter that image so it doesn't look like you have cloned a goat over and over. You can create some great flower bouquets from only a few flowers by copying and pasting. Add to that the ability to rotate, scale, and move the parts around so it looks like a just-picked bouquet.

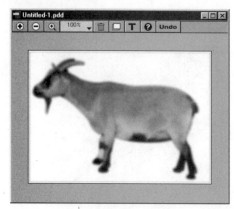

Figure 41. The goat image is blurry.

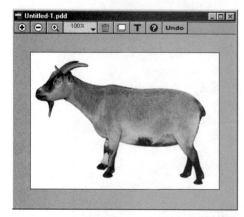

Figure 42. The Sharpen button cleared up Mr. Fuzzy Goat.

Figure 43. The background is muddy looking.

Figure 44. Instant Fix can clear up a dark image.

11. Click the Quality tab.

12. Click the Instant Fix button to fix the image (Figure 44).

13. Click the Edit tab.

14. Click the Paste button to paste in the goat.

15. Resize and reposition the goat in the foreground (Figure 45).

16. You can paste in more goats to create a herd (Figure 46).

Figure 45. The goat is on its own layer.

Figure 46. A herd of goats graze in front of the castle.

Using Combined Effects

Removing elements from photos and adding others

Before. The original image was a photo Ted took of Jen as she was being whisked away by an unlicensed parasailing outfit somewhere in Mexico.

After. We cloned away Jen, the motorboat pulling her, and the beach dude. Now the scene is quiet, and perfect for an alien invasion.

Uh-oh. We had a photo of a spaceship from a vacation. After removing the background, we copied the image and pasted it into this scene. Using the Paintbrush tool, we added the afterburner effect to the back of the flying ships, and a shadow to the one that landed.

Special Effects and Changing Colors

Before. *The original image of this butterfly was taken from a PhotoCD collection.*

After. *Crystallize was applied, the image was copied to another layer, and then Find Edges was applied to the copy. The result is outlined crystals.*

Bottom: *Sliding the Hue slider in the Hue/Saturation dialog box changed the color of the butterfly, but left all the detail intact.*

Correcting Dark Images

Before. The original image was quite dark, with no difference between the cat and the background. Variations will fix the color, while Sharpen and a bit of color adjustment is needed to fix Jerry. The cat doesn't want to be fixed.

After. Jerry's looking quite sharp (despite the goofy smile), and the background has been lightened a bit. Note that the color has also been adjusted slightly, providing a cure for Jerry's jaundice.

Before. This picture was taken when 110 film was still in the testing stage. At least, that's the excuse Ted's mom uses. We decided to run PhotoDeluxe's Instant Fix on the image instead of goofing around with other color correction tools.

After. Instant Fix did make a substantial improvement to the image, but a few problems remain: (1) the image has been over sharpened, (2) the shadows (especially the tree) are still too dark, and (3) who the heck dressed these kids?

Correcting an overexposed photograph

Before. *This photo came back partially overexposed. The red hues don't do the Charlie Brown-like tree justice. Of course, nothing could do that mirror justice, but we'll try nonetheless.*

After. *This required some work. First, we brought the image into Variations to try to reduce the red. Then we applied Instant Fix. The image is still far from perfect, but looks much better than the original.*

Adding clarity to a fuzzy image

Before. *Christmas in Pennsylvania can be quite dreary, but it should look better than this.*

After. *Using Sharpen and Brightness/Contrast, the detail of the trees and the whiteness of the snow stands out. Even the glare on the storm door is clear.*

Color correction on dull images

Before. *The original photograph is kind of lifeless, despite the fear of the owners that the house might be haunted.*

After. *Extensive use of Variations brings fuller color to the image. The sky was turned blue by selecting it with the Color Wand and using Variations on the highlights of the image.*

Creating Collages

The five images shown to the right were combined in PhotoDexluxe by copying and pasting them into one document. In order to drop the backgrounds of the flying flag and fireworks, we selected the background and deleted it from each layer.

We used Brightness/Contrast to darken the background flag. We also changed the color of the middle fireworks explosion to green to give the image some extra visual excitement.

Fixing an image and applying special effects

Before. Static the attack cat looks a little washed out in the original image.

After. Extensis Intellihance restores Static (and the background) to his colorful self.

Variation. We applied the Crackle filter to the background which provides a contrasting texture to Static's fur.

Variation. By playing with Brightness/Contrast, you can achieve a black light effect with any image.

Combining photographs

To combine these two images, the scorpion was selected, copied, and pasted into the document with the cactus (on a new layer). The cactus and some of the scrub were selected and copied to a new layer, which was moved in front of the scorpion layer. A shadow was added to the mountain area to make the scorpion blend in more with his new surroundings.

Fixing red eye

Before. In the original image, Erin and Jake have red eyes from the flash of the camera.

After. PhotoDeluxe's Red Eye function removes the red eye better than a six pack of Visine.

Creating a soft edge

Before. A lovely wedding photo for a lovely couple.

After. The lovely photo is now surrounded by a lovely feathered background, accomplished by creating an oval selection, feathering it, inverting the selection, and then pressing the lovely Delete key.

Red Eye Removal/Creating a Soft Edge

COMBINING PHOTOGRAPHS

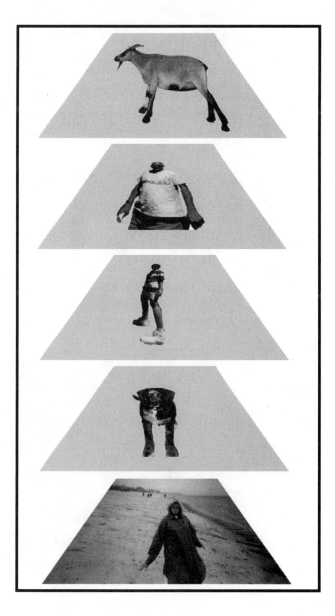

TAKING two images and combining them somehow. It's what the *Enquirer* does to sell papers. It's what O.J. claimed was done to the dozens of photos that show how comfortable those Bruno Magli's were before they had bloodstains and he had to throw them out in a dumpster in Chicago.

PhotoDeluxe provides some incredible tools for combining portions of images. Now you can convince little Bobby that alien spaceships do indeed hover over the house, and that they could suck him up and take him away at any time if he doesn't eat every last one of his lima beans (personally, we'd rather be abducted).

In some cases, no one will be able to tell that the image they're looking at has been altered. In other cases, certain attributes within an image conflict with other attributes (such as the direction, color, and intensity of light sources); these differences might be overlooked at first, but upon closer inspection they'll become obvious.

This chapter provides a number of examples and techniques to make the most of combining photos.

Using Layers

Layers can be compared to collages. When you add an object to an existing image, the new object will go on its own layer. That means the original image becomes the bottom layer, and the new object falls on the next layer up. New layers are numbered in order, such as Layer 1, Layer 2, etc. You can move a layer above or below another layer by dragging the layer name above or below another layer in the Layers palette. To activate a layer, you simply click on the layer's name. The active layer appears as a white bar, and the inactive layers appear as gray bars.

To combine a few basic elements:

1. Open a background image (Figure 1).

2. Open the image you want to add to the background image (Figure 2).

3. From the second image, select the object you want to add to the background image.

4. Choose Edit⇨Copy.

5. Return to the background image by choosing the name of the background image from the Window menu.

6. Choose Edit⇨Paste.

7. Resize the image as needed (Figure 3).

TIPS & TECHNIQUES

To merge a layer, click on the arrow in the upper right of the Layers window and drag to Merge layers. This will make all of your separate layers into one layer, with the exception of text. Text always remains on its own layer.

Figure 1. The original image looks so inviting.

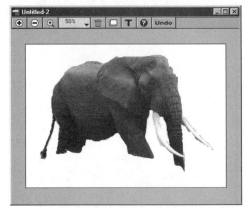

Figure 2. The elephant looks a little warm.

Figure 3. The two images are combined, keeping the elephant comfortable and displacing marginally enough water to flood the neighborhood.

Figure 4. The original image shows the goat behind mom.

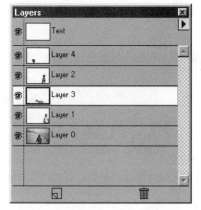

Figure 5. When you drag a layer on top of another, the object moves to the front of the image.

Figure 6. The goat is now in front of mom.

To move a layer:

1. Open the layered image (**Figure 4**).

2. In the Layers palette, click on the layer and drag it above another layer.

   Layer 3 in Figure 4 was dragged above Layer 1 to bring the goat in front of the woman (**Figure 5**).

3. You can also click on the image you want to move, and click and hold on the two layers (Figure 6) and choose: Send To Back, Send Back One, Bring Forward One, or Bring To Front (Figure 7).

> Send To Back
>
> Send Back One
>
> Bring Forward One
>
> Bring To Front

Figure 7. You have four choices for moving a selected layer.

TIPS & TECHNIQUES

To delete a layer, click on the object in that layer and press the Delete or Backspace key. You can also click and drag the layer you want to delete into the little trashcan in the Layers window. A third way to delete a layer is to click the layer to activate it, then choose Delete Layer from the Layers palette pop-up menu (in the upper-right corner of the Layers palette.

Text and layers

Text is automatically placed on its own layer. In the Layers window you'll see Layer 0 (your original image) and Text. Every document you open will have those two layers. Working with text in PhotoDeluxe is wonderful. You can always edit the text, even if you merge layers, because when you merge all of the layers, the text remains on its own layer.

To add text to an image:

1. Open the image to which you want to add text (Figure 8).

2. Click the T icon at the top of the image's window.

3. Enter the type, font, alignment, and color in the Text Tool dialog box (Figure 9).

4. Click the OK button to accept the type.

5. You can resize, rotate, or move the type using the handles around the outside of the type.

   Figure 10 shows the type in its final position.

Figure 8. The original image is just screaming for text.

Figure 9. The Text Tool dialog box lets you choose the font, alignment and color.

Figure 10. The type can be resized proportionately or disproportionately.

Figure 11. The original background image lacks people.

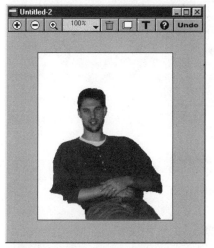

Figure 12. Here's Ted ready and waiting to be transported to a nicer atmosphere.

Figure 13. Ted on the cruise ship, looking quite natural.

To combine an image with a new background:

1. Open the image you want to use as a background (Figure 11).

2. Open the image with the person or object you want to add to the background (Figure 12).

   You can only open more than one image at a time if your preferences are set to open multiple images (see Chapter 2: PhotoDeluxe Basics).

3. Select only the person or object with your selection tools.

4. Choose Edit⇨Copy.

5. Go back to the background image and choose Edit⇨Paste.

6. Resize the image if needed (Figure 13).

TIPS & TECHNIQUES

Don't be fooled by the Paste Into function. When you choose Paste Into from the Edit menu, it will paste the copied image into the selected area, but not onto an individual layer. Paste puts the copied image onto its own layer.

To combine multiple elements:

1. Open your background image (Figure 14).

2. Open the image you want to add.

3. Choose Edit⇨Copy.

4. Go back to the background image and choose Edit⇨Paste.

5. Resize the added image if necessary (Figure 15).

6. Open another image that you want to add.

7. Choose Edit⇨Copy.

8. Go back to the background image and choose Edit⇨Paste.

9. Resize the added image if necessary.

10. Repeat the above steps until all of the new elements are added (Figure 16).

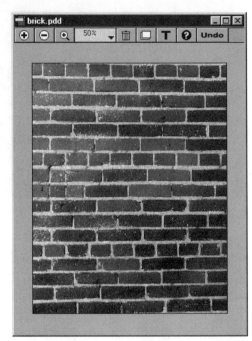

Figure 14. The background image is quite boring.

Figure 16. After all the images were in place, we added a dark rim around the necks using the Brush tool.

Figure 15. A head appears mounted on the brick wall.

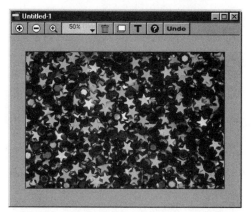

Figure 17. The background texture is a bunch of stars.

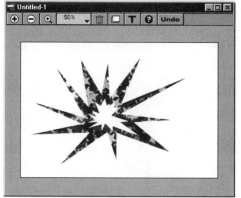

Figure 18. The Paste Into function puts the cut image within the selection.

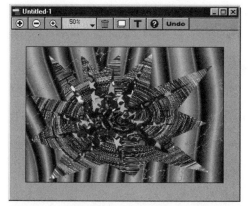

Figure 19. The finished image shows a multitude of patterns create by combining multiple selections.

To create a kaleidoscope effect using selections:

1. Open a background texture (Figure 17).

2. Choose Edit⇨Select All.

3. Choose Edit⇨Cut.

4. Create a polygonal selection using the Polygon tool.

5. Choose Edit⇨Paste Into (Figure 18).

6. Create a new layer by clicking the arrow in the upper-right corner of the Layers palette (which displays a pop-up menu) and selecting New Layer from that menu.

7. Repeat steps 1 through 6 with different images until you achieve a kaleidoscope effect (Figure 19).

Creating a Kaleidoscope

TIPS & TECHNIQUES

Instead of choosing Cut from the Edit menu, right-click with the mouse and choose Cut from the menu that appears.

To combine different heads with bodies:

1. Open the image you want to alter (Figure 20).

2. In this example, open the image with the head you want to use (Figure 21).

3. Copy only the head and paste it into the first image aligning with the body.

4. Resize as needed.

5. Select the parts of the neck you want to delete by using the Trace tool and then press the Delete key. (Figure 22).

   Using layers and sections of images can be quite fun. Just think of all of those photos you have and the things you can do to your friends and relatives. Hopefully they all have a sense of humor.

Figure 20. Ted's head could use a little improvement.

Figure 21. Janus the Ostrich volunteers his services.

Figure 22. After the photo surgery, Ted developed an odd urge to stick his head in the sand.

Altering People and Objects

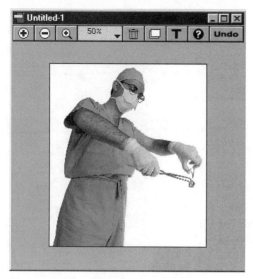

Figure 23. The original image shows a doctor waiting for his patient.

To combine differently sized images:

1. Open the image you want to use as the background or base (Figure 23).

2. Open a larger image that you want to add to the original.

3. Select a portion using one or more selection tools, or select the entire image and choose Edit⇨Copy.

4. View the background image and choose Edit⇨Paste.

5. The added image is significantly larger, so you'll need to make it smaller by dragging one of the corner handles inward (Figure 24).

6. Move and resize the image, then press Enter to accept the new size.

7. Add another image and resize to finish your photo (Figure 25).

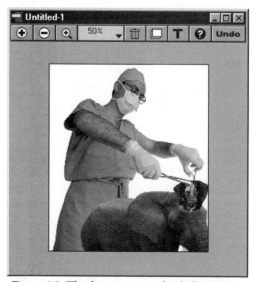

Figure 24. A quick check behind the ears occurs when the image is placed.

Figure 25. The doctor removes the elephant's brain, which looks suspiciously like the head of a dog.

Combing Different-Sized Images

To change a background:

1. Open an image that you wish to use as a background (Figure 26).

2. Using your Selection tools, select only the sky from that image.

   Because our image had a fairly consistent color and tone, we used the Color Wand to select the sky with a single click.

3. Create a new layer by clicking the paper icon in the Layers palette.

4. Open another image that you want to use as your sky (Figure 27).

5. Select the whole image by choosing Select⇨All.

6. Choose Edit⇨Copy.

7. Go back to the original image and choose Edit⇨Paste Into (Figure 28).

   Since you created a layer (in Step 3), it is easy to get rid of the new sky if you don't like it.

Figure 26. The original sky is bland and dull.

Figure 27. This image has a much more interesting sky.

Figure 28. The new sky adds some visual interest to the background of the church.

CREATING A BUSINESS IDENTITY

YOU can use PhotoDeluxe to create complex materials to promote your business. For instance, you can create and modify a logo, and incorporate it within one of several templates.

In this way, you can add not only designs (like those created in a drawing program like Adobe Illustrator), but photographs to your logo and business materials. Even if you don't have a business, you can use some of PhotoDeluxe's capabilities to create all sorts of cards and posters.

Logo creation

Creating a logo starts with an idea. A sketch can be helpful to get you started. That sketch can be scanned into PhotoDeluxe and modified from there. The following steps take you through the process of creating a very basic logo. Of course, you can be as creative as you want when using PhotoDeluxe to create a logo (but we only have so much room on a page here...).

To create a basic logo:

1. Choose File⟹New to create a new document that is 7 inches by 7 inches (Figure 1).

2. Using the Selection tools, create a selection to fill with color to use as your logo (Figure 2).

3. After creating your selection, press Alt+Delete (Option-Delete) to fill the selection with black (Figure 3).

4. Create a dot and fill with a color.

5. Select both the dot and the original shape.

6. Choose Edit⟹Copy, then choose Edit⟹Paste.

7. Click the Advanced button.

8. Click the Orientation tab.

9. Click the Flip Vertical button.

    This creates a flipped copy of the original.

10. Move the flipped copy below the original to form your design.

11. Change one dot and one half circle to be a gray color using the Color change button (Figure 4).

Figure 1. For this new file, we created a 7 by 7 inch document.

Figure 2. By using the Circle tool with the Rectangle tool you can create a variety of selections.

Figure 3. The fill will be black unless you have changed the foreground color.

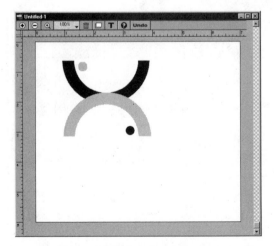

Figure 4. The logo has a ying-yang quality to it.

Figure 5. The file is ready for exporting.

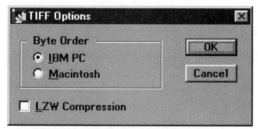

Figure 6. The Export dialog box is where you choose where you save to, the file name, and the type of file.

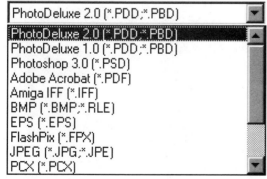

Figure 7. If you are working on a PC, you must choose IBM PC or you won't be able to open the file.

Placing PhotoDeluxe images in other programs

Any image you create in PhotoDeluxe can be used in other programs. First, export the file from PhotoDeluxe, and it will be ready for placement in another program. In that other program, you can add type, create a layout, and more. Check with your other application's documentation to see what types of image formats can be placed into documents. As a general guideline, use TIFF if you'll be printing and either JPEG or GIF89a for the screen.

To export an image to another program:

1. Open the image you want to export (Figure 5).

2. Click the Send button.

3. Click the To Disk tab.

4. Click the Export button.

5. Click the Export tab.

6. Click the Other Export button to access the Export dialog box (Figure 6).

   After you've chosen the file type (we chose TIFF) and click OK, a dialog box will appear with additional options in it (Figure 7).

7. If you choose to export in TIFF format, choose IBM PC or Macintosh.

8. Click the OK button.

TIPS & TECHNIQUES

To export an image you can also choose File⇨Send To⇨File Format. This will bring up the Save As dialog box giving you a plethora of choices in which to save your file (Figure 8).

Figure 8. You can scroll down to see more file format choices.

Placing Images in Other Programs

PhotoDeluxe provides templates that allow you to create your own labels. You can choose CD, floppy disk, name tags, stickers, video labels and more.

To create a label:

1. Click the Cards & More button.
2. Click the Labels tab.
3. Click the Labels button.
4. Click the Choose Label tab.
5. Click the Choose Label button.

   This opens the Templates window for you to choose a label template (**Figure 9**).

6. Double-click on a template.

   This opens up the template for you to add a photo and edit text (**Figure 10**).

7. Click on the Add tab.
8. Click the Open File and double-click on the image you want to add to your label.
9. Double-click on the text to edit it.
10. Click the Done button to finish the labels (Figure 11).

Figure 9. The Templates window lets you choose a wide variety of labels.

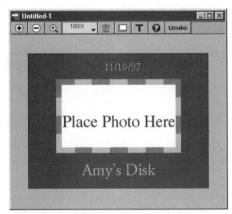

Figure 10. The template is ready for editing.

Figure 11. The final label is ready to be printed on sticky label sheets.

Creating Labels

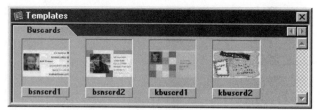

Figure 11. The Templates window gives you four choices of preset templates for business cards or you can create your own.

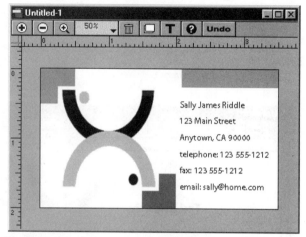

Figure 12. The logo we created earlier fits this card nicely.

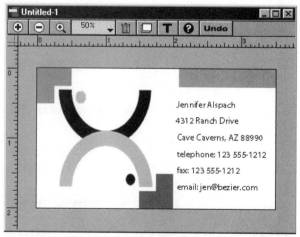

Figure 13. The final card shows all the correct information on this business card (yeah, right).

To create a business card:

1. Click the Cards & More button.

2. Click the Cards & Calendars tab.

3. Click the Business Cards button.

4. Click the Choose Business Card tab.

5. Click the Choose Card button.

   This brings up the Templates window from which you can choose a layout (**Figure 11**).

6. Double-click on a layout to open that card template.

7. Click the Add tab to add your photo or logo.

   You have the choice of using your own photos, sample photos, clip art, or art from your camera, scanner, disc/CD, Internet, or other.

8. Choose Open File and open the logo you created earlier in this chapter (Figure 12).

9. Resize the image if needed.

10. Double-click on the text to edit the type.

11. Click the Done button to finish the card (Figure 13).

To create letterhead:

1. Click the Cards & More button.

2. Click the Pages tab.

3. Click the Stationery button.

4. Click the Choose Stationery tab.

5. Click the Choose Stationery button.

   This brings up the Templates window from which you can choose a template.

6. Double-click on a letterhead you want to use (Figure 14).

7. Click the Add tab to add your photo or logo.

   You have the choice of using photos, sample photos, clip art, or art from a camera, scanner, disc/CD, Internet, or other.

8. Choose Open File and open the logo you created earlier in this chapter (Figure 15).

9. Resize the image if needed.

10. Double-click on the text to edit the type.

11. Click the Done button to finish the card (Figure 16).

Figure 14. The Template window gives you four choices of stationery.

Figure 15. The logo we created earlier works great for stationery.

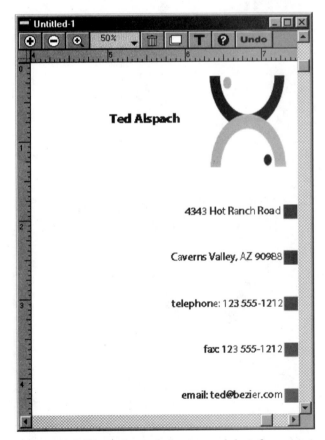

Figure 16. The stationery looks great and the information is now accurate.

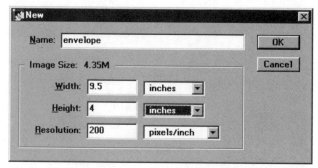

Figure 17. The logo can be sized to fit the envelope.

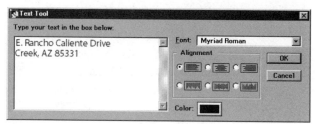

Figure 18. The Text Tool dialog box is where you enter the font, alignment, and color of the type.

Figure 19. The finished envelope is ready for printing.

To create an envelope:

1. Choose File⇨New.

    The New dialog box appears.

2. Enter the name of the file, the width as 9-1/2 inches and the height as 4 inches. Choose the resolution you need for the printer you are using (Figure 17).

    For more information about resolution, see Chapter 2: PhotoDeluxe Basics.

3. Click the OK button.

4. Choose File⇨Open File and double-click on the logo you created earlier.

    If you cannot open more than one file, choose File⇨Preferences, and check the Allow Multiple Document Windows option.

5. Click the Advanced button to access the advanced pull-down menus.

6. Choose Select⇨All to select the whole logo.

7. Choose Edit⇨Copy.

8. Go back to the Envelope document and choose Edit⇨Paste.

9. Resize the logo to fit the left side of the envelope.

10. Click the T logo at the top of the Envelope Document window to access the Text Tool dialog box (Figure 18).

11. Enter the return address. Choose the font, alignment, and color.

    When you press the Return key in the Text Tool window, you actually create a new line by adding a carriage return.

12. Click the OK button.

13. Move and resize the type to fit above the logo (Figure 19).

To create a sign:

1. Click the Cards & More button.

2. Click the Pages tab.

3. Click the Signs button.

4. Click the Choose Sign tab.

5. Click the Choose Sign button to access the Templates window (Figure 20).

6. Choose a sign template by double-clicking on it.

7. Click the Add tab to add your logo.

8. Choose File⇨Open File and double-click on the logo you created at the beginning of this chapter.

9. Resize the logo to fit the area of the sign (Figure 21).

10. Double-click on the type to edit it.

11. Click the OK button when the type is correct (Figure 22).

12. Click the Done button to end the activity.

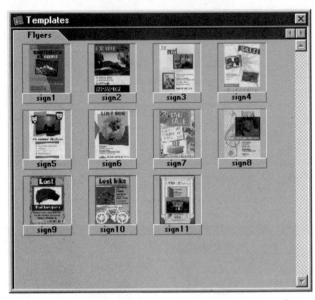

Figure 20. The Templates window lets you choose from a number of sign templates.

Figure 22. The finished sign is ready for printing and distribution.

Figure 21. The image is added to the template (with the template text).

Creating Signs

Figure 23. The Templates window gives you three standard certificate choices.

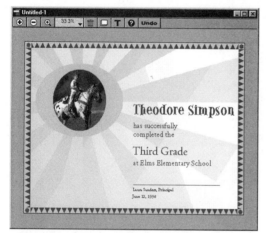

Figure 24. Here we've added our photo to the certificate template (but haven't changed the text).

Figure 25. After changing the text, the final certificate looks almost legal.

PhotoDeluxe's certificate templates allow you to create different types of certificates, including special awards and coupons. It's a great way to boost morale within your company. Just think, you could create a certificate to give to the person who takes the shortest lunch, who pads their expense account the least, and who has (so far) never been caught stealing office supplies.

To create a certificate:

1. Click the Cards & More button.
2. Click the Pages tab.
3. Click the Certificates button.
4. Click the Choose Certificate tab.
5. Click the Choose Certificate button.

   This brings up the Templates window (**Figure 23**).
6. Choose a certificate by double-clicking on it.

   This opens up the template for you to add photos and edit the text.
7. Click the Add tab.
8. Click the Open File button and choose a photo for your certificate (Figure 24).
9. Resize the photo if needed.
10. Double-click on the text to edit the text.
11. Click the Done tab to finish the certificate (Figure 25).

TEXTURES AND 3D EFFECTS

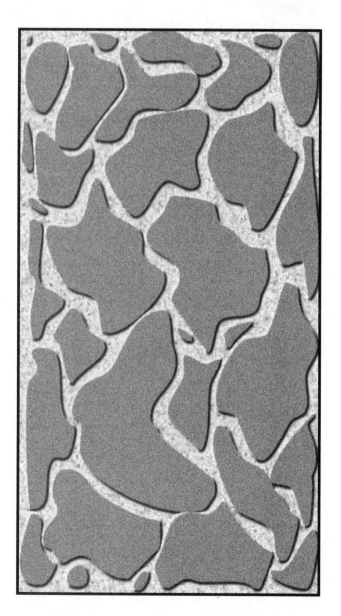

THE number of textures that can be added to images using PhotoDeluxe is limitless, thanks to several features built right into the program.

You can create a texture from an existing object, or from nothing at all. Further, you can create a texture in a selection, so that only a portion of an image has a texture applied to it. Textures can be used as backgrounds, as "filler," or for any other purpose you deem them suitable for.

PhotoDeluxe also has several features that allow you to make your images appear to pop into the 3D world, such as creating a drop shadow for a portion of your image.

To create a swirl texture from a solid color:

1. Choose File⇨New.

   The New dialog box appears (Figure 1).

2. Enter a name for the file, a size, and a resolution.

3. Click the Advanced button.

   This takes you to the advanced areas.

4. Click the Tools tab.

5. Click the Color Change button.

   With the Color Change button, you can change the forground and background colors.

6. Click the Color button in the Color Change dialog box to pick a new color.

7. Click the eyedropper in the colored area to pick a color.

8. Click the OK button.

9. While holding the Alt (Option) key, press the Backspace or Delete key.

   This will fill in the selected area (or the entire image if you haven't selected anything) with the color you have chosen.

10. Choose Select⇨None.

11. Click the Effects tab.

12. Click the Special Effects button.

13. Click the Blur tab.

14. Click the Noise button to activate the Noise dialog box (Figure 2).

    Noise automatically gives your plain background a little texture.

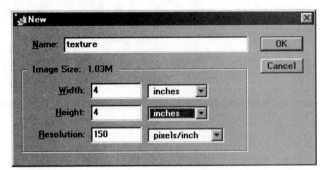

Figure 1. The New dialog box lets you choose the name, size, and resolution of your document.

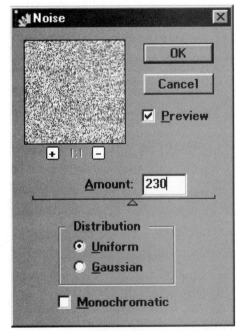

Figure 2. The Noise dialog box lets you see a preview before you click the OK button.

Creating a Swirl Texture

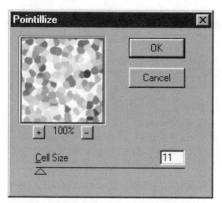

Figure 3. The Pointillize effect makes circular-shaped cells from your image.

Figure 4. The Twirl effect makes things look like they are going down the drain.

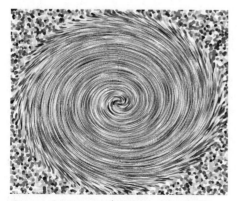

Figure 5. It is amazing to see that you can create a texture from an empty document.

15. **Set the Amount to 230 and the Distribution to Uniform.**

    The higher the value in the Amount field, the more "noise" will be generated. Picking Uniform instead of Gaussian results in more even distribution of light and dark areas.

16. **Click the OK button.**

17. **Click the Artistic tab.**

18. **Click the Pointillize button to activate the Pointillize dialog box (Figure 3).**

    The Pointillize button creates circular textures from the noise that you created.

19. **Change the Cell Size to 8.**

    The larger the Cell Size, the bigger the cells will be.

20. **Click the OK button.**

21. **Click the Fun tab.**

22. **Click the Twirl button to activate the Twirl dialog box (Figure 4).**

23. **Enter the number 833 for the Angle so you get a massive twirl.**

    The lower the Angle number, the less the twirl. The higher the number, the greater the twirl (up to 999).

24. **Click the OK button.**

25. **Click the Advanced button twice to get back to the Advanced tabs.**

26. **Click the Size tab.**

27. **Click the Trim button to cut away any of the image that didn't twirl.**

28. **Drag a marquee around the part you want to keep.**

    You can resize the marquee by dragging one of the corner handles until you get the size you want.

29. **Hit the Return key to see the results (Figure 5).**

Creating a Swirl Texture

To create a texture for a text background:

1. Choose File⇨New.

    The New dialog box appears.

2. Enter a name for the file, a size, and a resolution (Figure 6).

3. Click the Advanced button.

4. Click the Tools tab.

    The Tools tab lets you work with the Brush, Color Change, Line, Eraser, Smudge and Clone tools.

5. Click the Color Change button.

6. Click the Color button in the Color Picker dialog box to pick a new color (Figure 7).

7. Click the eyedropper in the colored area to pick a color.

8. Click the OK button.

9. While holding the Alt (Option) key, press the Backspace or Delete key (Figure 8).

    This fills in the area with the color you have chosen.

    You can access color swatches by double-clicking on the Foreground color swatch, then clicking the Define Custom Colors button.

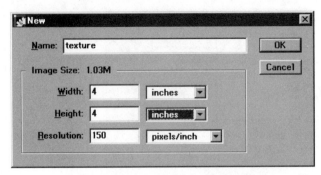

Figure 6. The New dialog box will always create a white background after you click the OK button.

Figure 7. The Color Picker dialog box lets you pick a color with an eyedropper.

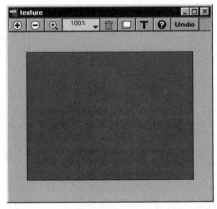

Figure 8. When you press Alt+Delete (Option-Delete) the white background fills with your new foreground color.

Figure 9. The Merge Clouds effect also works well for a sky.

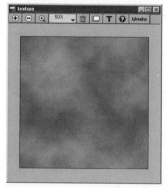

Figure 10. The Brightness slider in the Brightness/Contrast dialog box makes the image light enough to read text through.

Once upon a time there lived a troll. The troll's name was Horace. He lived under a bridge.

Figure 11. Black type on top of the image is easily visible.

10. Choose Select⇨None.

11. Click the Effects tab.

12. Click the Special Effects button.

13. Click the Cool tab.

14. Click the Merge Clouds button.

    This will create a cloud effect from the colors you choose as foreground and background (**Figure 9**).

15. Click the Done tab.

16. Click the Quality tab.

17. Click the **Brightness/Contrast** button.

    This activates the Brightness/ Contrast dialog box so you can see the effect as you drag the sliders.

18. **Increase the Brightness control so you'll be able to see type over the image (Figure 10).**

19. **Click the T icon at the top of the document window to add type (Figure 11).**

TIPS & TECHNIQUES

If you keep clicking the Merge Clouds button PhotoDeluxe will cycle through different cloud formations until you find one you like.

Creating Stucco Textures

To create a stucco texture from a photo:

1. Open the photo you want to create a texture from (Figure 12).

2. Click the Advanced button.

   This will access the Advanced features.

3. Click the Effects tab.

4. Click the Special Effects button.

   This will access the Artistic, Fun, Blur, Cool, and Cooler effects.

5. Click the Cooler tab.

6. Click the Colored Pencil button.

   This opens the Colored Pencil dialog box where you can get a rough idea of what the effect will look like in its preview box (**Figure 13**).

7. Click the OK button to create the colored pencil effect.

8. Click the Crackle button.

   This opens the Crackle dialog box (Figure 14).

9. Click the OK button to see the final effect, then click the Done tab (Figure 15).

Figure 12. The original photo has plenty of colors which will make a great texture.

Figure 13. The Colored Pencil dialog box lets you see a preview before you click OK.

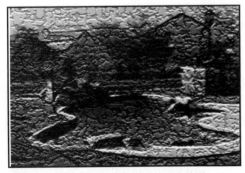

Figure 15. The final image is rich with texture.

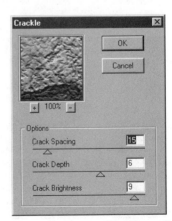

Figure 14. The Crackle effect will create a stucco effect on your image.

Figure 16. The original image has lots of color.

Figure 17. The Ripple dialog box lets you preview the effect before you click OK.

Figure 18. The final image looks spiky and textured.

To create a shocked effect with a photo:

1. Open a photo with plenty of color (**Figure 16**).

   An image with lots of color will make a rich texture.

2. Click the Advanced button.

3. Click the Effects tab.

4. Click the Special Effects button.

5. Click the Fun tab.

6. Click the Ripple button.

   This opens the Ripple dialog box (**Figure 17**). You can zoom out from the Ripple dialog box to see the whole image before you click the OK button.

7. Set the amount to a large number. We chose 889.

8. Set the Size to Large.

   The small size would make a slight ripple. A medium setting would ripple a little more. A large setting would create an even larger-looking ripple effect.

9. Click the OK button to see the effect (**Figure 18**).

10. Click the Done tab to exit the activity.

To create a shadow:

1. Open an image you want to shadow (Figure 19).

2. Click the Advanced button.

3. Choose View⇨Show Layers.

4. Click on the layer you want to add the shadow to (Figure 20).

   If your object isn't layered, then create a selection around the object you want to make a shadow on.

5. Click the Effects tab.

6. Choose Select⇨All.

7. Click the Drop Shadow button to activate the Drop Shadow dialog box (Figure 21).

8. Choose an Offset, Direction, Fill Color, and the Fill Opacity.

   Offset controls how far the shadow is from the source.

   Fill Color is the color of the shadow itself.

   Fill Opacity is how opaque (not transparent) the shadow is. The higher the percentage, the less transparent the shadow will be, obscuring more of the background.

   Anytime you create a shadow it automatically goes on its own layer. That way it is easy to select if you want to delete it or soften it.

Figure 19. The original image is obviously two combined photos.

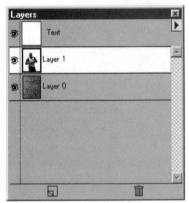

Figure 20. In the Layers palette you can activate a layer by clicking on the name of the layer.

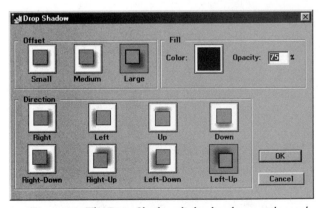

Figure 21. The Drop Shadow dialog box lets you choose the offset, direction, fill color, and opacity of the shadow.

Figure 22. The shadow looks much too harsh to be realistic.

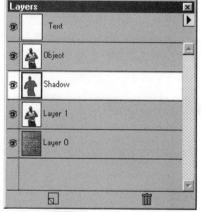

Figure 23. The Layers palette lets you activate layers, delete them, or make them visible.

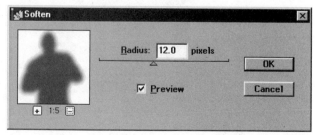

Figure 24. The Soften dialog box lets you preview the softened edges before you click OK.

9. Click the OK button to see the shadow (Figure 22).

10. Click on the Shadow layer to activate that layer (Figure 23).

11. Click the Special Effects button.

12. Click the Blur tab.

13. Click the Soften button to open the Soften dialog box (Figure 24).

14. Drag the Radius slider until you like the shadow's edges.

15. Click the OK button to see the final shadow (Figure 25).

16. Click the Done tab to end the activity.

Figure 25. The final image looks like the basketball player was standing in front of the brick wall just as someone took his picture with a flash.

Creating a Shadow

To curl up the corner of a photo:

1. Open the image whose corner you'd like to curl (Figure 26).

2. Click the Advanced button.

3. Click the Effects tab.

4. Click the Special Effects button.

5. Click the Cool Tab.

   This activates some of the more unusual effects.

6. Click the Page Curl button.

   This creates an automatic page curl on your image. The background behind the page will fill with your foreground color, which in this case was black (**Figure 27**).

   The curl itself will appear slightly transparent, allowing you to see part of the image behind it. The curl affects the lower right of the image each time it is applied.

Figure 26. The original image of Harvey looks fine, but the picture is flat.

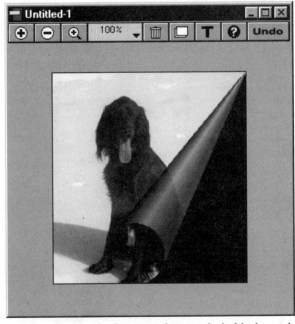

Figure 27. The final picture of Harvey looks like he might need a bit of moisturizer (he's peeling, you see).

TIPS & TECHNIQUES

You can curl *any* corner of the image using Page Curl. Before you apply it, rotate and/or flip the image (using the Options in the Orientation menu after you've clicked the Advanced button). Using this method, you can curl more than one corner of the image at once.

Curling the Corner of a Photo

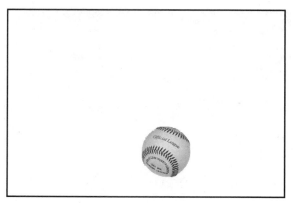

Figure 28. The original baseball is so lonely.

Figure 29. The football is easily moved behind the baseball.

Figure 30. The soccer ball is moved to the back by dragging a layer.

To give the illusion of depth to an image:

1. Open an image to combine with another image (Figure 28).

2. Open a second image and select just the object, using your selection tools.

3. Choose Edit⇨Copy.

4. Go back to the original image and choose Edit⇨Paste.

5. Choose View⇨Show Layers.

6. In the Layers palette drag the baseball layer (Layer 0) on top of the football layer (Layer 1) to move the baseball back to the front (Figure 29).

7. Open another image and select only one object.

8. Choose Edit⇨Copy, go back to the original image and choose Edit⇨Paste.

9. In the Layers palette drag the soccer layer (Layer 2) to the bottom of the Layers palette (Figure 30).

   It is easy to create a sense of depth by moving the layers around. It is even more believable when the objects have shadows (see the next page).

Creating Depth

TIPS & TECHNIQUES

You can have unlimited layers in PhotoDeluxe. Keep in mind, however, that each layer uses memory; the more layers you use, the slower PhotoDeluxe will run.

145

To create a shadow on the image:

1. Open the layered image you created on the previous page.

2. Click the Advanced button.

3. Choose View⇨Show Layers.

4. Click on the baseball layer to activate it.

   The layer needs to be active for you to select the baseball.

5. Choose⇨Select All.

6. Click the Effects tab.

7. Click the Drop Shadow button.

   This opens the Drop Shadow dialog box (**Figure 31**).

8. Choose a large shadow with the direction going above the source, make the fill color black, and set the opacity to 85%.

9. Click the Shadow layer to activate that layer.

10. Click the Special Effects button.

11. Click the Blur tab.

12. Click the Soften button to activate the Soften dialog box.

13. Click the OK button to see the shadow created from the baseball on the football (Figure 32).

14. Repeat steps 2 through 13 on the football layer.

15. Click the Done button to end the activity

    The final result is shown in Figure 33.

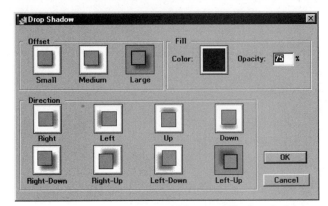

Figure 31. The Drop Shadow dialog box.

Figure 32. The baseball casts a shadow on the football.

Figure 33. The final image shows the shadow on the foremost objects.

BACKGROUND MANIPULATION

THE background of an image is often as important (if not more so) as the foreground of an image. Careful background manipulation is the key to making photographs look their best, whether you want that background to be as vivid and noticeable as the foreground subject(s), or whether you want the background to make the foreground "pop out" of the image.

PhotoDeluxe lets you adjust the background in several different ways, from working with an original background image that's on its own layer, to adjusting the background that's around the foreground image by careful selection methods. The following pages describe different techniques to make your backgrounds work exactly the way you want them to.

To remove a background:

1. Open the image from which you want to remove the background (Figure 1).

2. Click the Advanced button.

3. Choose View⇨Show Selections from the pull-down menu.

4. Choose the SmartSelect tool.

   This tool will differentiate between colored pixels to draw the selection around your object. You can add and take away from the selection to make it perfect.

5. Carefully trace around the edge of your object and its background, or select the background itself (Figure 2).

   In some images, the background is easier to select than the object. In other images, the object may be easier to select. After you use the SmartSelect tool a number of times you'll begin to get a feel for which is easier to select.

6. If you selected the object, click the Invert button in the Selections dialog box to select only the background.

   If you selected the background, move on to the next step.

7. If you press the Delete key, the background will fill with white (Figure 3). If you press Alt+Delete (Option-Delete), it will fill the background with the foreground color you used last.

Figure 1. The sky background in this image isn't consistent enough for our needs.

Figure 2. The SmartSelect tool is a great tool to use to remove a background.

Figure 3. The white background will be a breeze to select later with the Color Wand.

Figure 4. This soccer ball appears to be resting comfortably atop the snow.

Figure 5. Choose a blue sky color for the foreground and white for the background.

Figure 6. This is Ted's view right after he connects with an upside-down flipping back kick.

To create a background with special effects:

1. Open the image that lacks a background (Figure 4).

2. Click the Advanced button.

3. Select only the background using the Color Wand.

4. Click the Invert button in the Selections window to select just the soccer ball.

5. Choose Edit⇨Cut.

6. Choose⇨Edit Paste.

    This puts the soccer ball on its own layer so you can change the whole background.

7. Click on Layer 1 to access the background layer.

8. Click the Tools tab.

9. Click the Color Change button.

    We'll need to pick a nice blue sky color to use with the Merge Clouds effect.

10. Using the eyedropper, pick a blue sky color for the foreground and white for the background (Figure 5).

11. Click the OK button.

12. Hold the Alt (Option) key while you press the Delete button to fill the background with blue.

13. Click the Effects tab.

14. Click the Special Effects button.

15. Click the Cool tab.

16. Click the Merge Clouds button (Figure 6).

    You may have to click the Merge Clouds button a few times until you see the cloud formation you like.

17. Click the Done tab.

To create a "paint by numbers" background:

1. Open a combined photo (Figure 7).

2. Click the Advanced button.

3. Click on the background layer to activate that layer.

4. Click the Effects tab.

5. Click the Special Effects button.

6. Click the Cooler tab.

7. Click the Sponge button to activate the Sponge dialog box (Figure 8).

   Take the time to play with the three sliders to see the different results. Different images can be affected in entirely different ways with the same settings.

8. **Click the OK button.**

   The final image shows an artist in front of his latest work (**Figure 9**).

Figure 7. The combined photo shows Ted in front of a picture of Sedona.

Figure 8. The Sponge dialog box lets you create a painterly effect on your layer.

Figure 9. None of us ever thought Ted had it in him to do such beautiful work.

Figure 10. The original image is two combined photos.

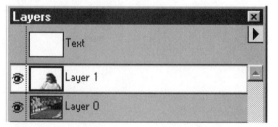

Figure 11. The Layers palette shows the separate images on their own layers.

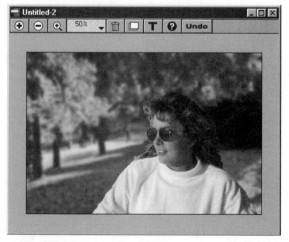

Figure 12. The person in the foreground really stands out against the blurred background.

To blur your background so the foreground stands out:

1. Open the image from which you want to blur the background (Figure 10).

2. Click the Advanced button.

3. Select only the background using any of the selection tools.

   This is easy if the background and the person are on separate layers (**Figure 11**). If they aren't on separate layers, select the background using one of the techniques presented in Chapter 4.

4. Click on the background layer to activate that layer.

5. Click the Effects tab.

6. Click the Special Effects button.

7. Click the Blur tab.

8. Click the Soften button to open the Soften dialog box.

9. Enter a low number for the Radius. We used 3.9 pixels.

   This makes the foreground image really pop out.

10. Click the OK button to see the final blurred background (Figure 12).

To add noise to a background so your foreground image stands out:

1. Open any image that you want to change (Figure 13).

2. Click the Advanced button.

3. Click on the sky layer to activate that layer.

   You'll know the layer is active because it appears white in the Layers palette.

4. Click the Effects tab.

5. Click the Special Effects button.

6. Click the Blur tab.

7. Click the Noise button to activate the Noise dialog box (Figure 14).

8. Set the Amount to 46 and the Distribution to Uniform.

   You'll want to leave the Monochromatic box unchecked so you get the full range of colors.

9. Click the OK button to accept the noise.

10. Click the Done tab to finish the image (Figure 15).

Figure 13. The original image could benefit from some texture in the background.

Figure 14. The Noise dialog box shows you a preview before you click the OK button.

Figure 15. The sky is now much more interesting and you can really see the foreground pop out.

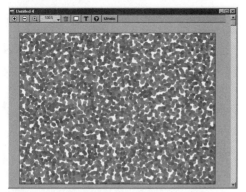

Figure 16. The Pointillize effect can create worm-like segments.

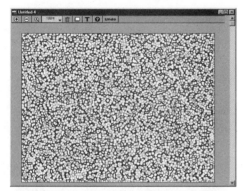

Figure 17. The Find Edges effect will outline the worm segments.

Figure 18. The Negative effect makes the lines bright and neon colored.

To create a texture for a background:

1. Create a new document that is approximately 4 inches across by 3 inches high.

2. Fill in the white area with a color using the Change Color button in the Tools tab.

3. Click the Advanced button.

4. Click the Effects button.

5. Click the Special Effects button.

6. Click the Artistic tab.

7. Click the Pointillize button to activate the Pointillize dialog box.

8. Set the Cell Size to 12 to create worm-like segments (Figure 16).

9. In the Artistic tab, click the Find Edges button to create an outlined effect (Figure 17).

10. Click the Fun tab.

11. Click the Negative button to create a bright neon background (Figure 18).

Creating Textured Backgrounds

To add a background to an object:

1. Open an image to add to a background (Figure 19).

2. From that image, select just the person or object you want to copy to a different background using any of the selection tools.

   Chapter 4 explains the use of each of the selection tools as well as various selection techniques.

3. Choose Edit⇨Copy.

4. Open a background image (Figure 20).

5. Choose Edit⇨Paste.

6. You may need to resize the image to fit the background (Figure 21).

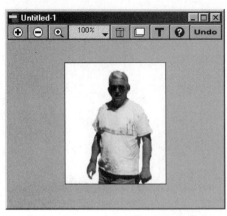

Figure 19. The handsome man in this picture lacks an interesting background.

Figure 20. This agave-filled photo is a perfect background image.

TIPS & TECHNIQUES

You may want to add a feather to soften the edge of the copied object by choosing the Advanced button, clicking the Effects tab, then clicking the Feather button. A slight feather of 1 or 2 pixels should be enough to provide a partially transparent selection edge.

Figure 21. This tourist is amazed at the size of the agave plants in Arizona.

Adding a Background to an Object

Figure 22. The white background in this image doesn't do this stunning spotted specimen justice.

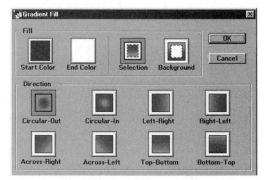

Figure 23. The Gradient Fill dialog offers you many choices.

Figure 24. The new background brings out the eyes in this giraffe (and illustrates his amazing psychic abilities).

To create a gradient for a background image:

1. Open the image that needs a background (Figure 22).

2. Click the Advanced button.

3. Using the Color Wand, select the white background.

4. Click the Effects tab.

5. Click the Gradient Fill button to activate the Gradient Fill dialog box (Figure 23).

6. Choose a Start and an End color.

7. Click the Selection button, so that the gradient appears within the selection.

8. Choose a direction from the eight options provided.

9. Click the OK button to see the effect (Figure 24).

Using Gradients as Backgrounds

TIPS & TECHNIQUES

To soften the edge between the object and the background, choose the Feather button before filling the gradient in the Effects tab. An amount of 1 to 2 pixels is usually enough.

COLOR CORRECTION

MAKING color images look their best is tricky business, but PhotoDeluxe makes it easier than in almost any other program.

Of course, this chapter (like the majority of this book) was printed in black and white, so you'll have to take our word for it that the images look better. Look at the color section of the book for specific examples on color correction using the different PhotoDeluxe tools.

Instant Fix

The Instant Fix button in the Advanced area can perform miracles on a photo taken with a cheap camera or it can fix up any bad photo. PhotoDeluxe's Instant Fix takes the guesswork out of cleaning up a photo.

To apply Instant Fix to a bad photo:

1. Open the muddy photo (Figure 1).

2. Click the Advanced button.

3. Click the Quality tab.

4. Click the Instant Fix button to see the transformation (Figure 2).

   Instant Fix is a great effect since it takes no effort or thought on the part of the user. You simply click the Instant Fix button and there you have it; your image looks perfect.

Figure 1. This photo is almost 30 years old, but can clean up quite well.

Figure 2. The transformation of the snowy scene is amazing.

Fixing Images Instantly

TIPS & TECHNIQUES

You can apply more than one effect to a photo to achieve a cleaner image. If Instant Fix isn't enough, you may want to try the Brightness/Contrast button to clean up the image a little more.

Figure 3. The original photo is overpowed with red and magenta colors.

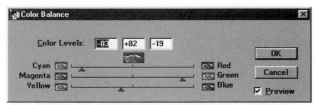

Figure 4. The Color Balance dialog box lets you fix the color cast.

Figure 5. The final image looks perfect, even if caught in the act.

Color Balance

When working with color images, the Color Balance effect is a great way to balance your colors. You look at which color is too strong, and add more of the opposite color.

To fix an image's color:

1. Open the photo that needs to be fixed (**Figure 3**).

2. Click the Advanced button.

3. Click the Quality tab.

4. Click the Color Balance button (**Figure 4**).

   This opens the Color Balance dialog box where you can adjust cyan, magenta, yellow, red, green, and blue values. You also see a preview before you click the OK button. If there is too much red in the image like in this photo, you need to drag the slider towards cyan to compensate. By dragging the opposite way of the overpowering color, you'll balance out the color.

5. Click the OK button.

   The image will display the changes you've made in the Color Balance dialog box (**Figure 5**).

Fixing Image Colors

159

To correct the Brightness and Contrast of an image:

1. Open the image that lacks contrast (Figure 6).

2. Click the Advanced button.

3. Click the Quality tab.

4. Click the **Brightness/Contrast** button (Figure 7).

   This activates the Brightness/ Contrast dialog box where you can adjust the brightness, contrast, or both.

5. **Click the OK button to see the results (Figure 8).**

   If this step isn't quite enough, you may want to use the Instant Fix, or the Sharpen button to clear up any blurriness.

   Page 102 and the color section show other examples of Brightness/Contrast adjustment

Figure 6. The original image has a overall gray tone, with no real contrast.

Figure 7. The Brightness/Contrast dialog box lets you adjust the dark and light tones of your image.

Figure 8. The final image shows these lovely women in a much clearer light.

Figure 9. The original image shows water that's gray, and a dull, lifeless background.

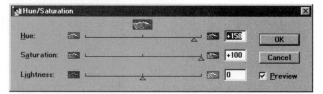

Figure 10. The Hue/Saturation dialog box lets you rotate Hue, increase or decrease the Saturation, and adjust the Lightness.

Figure 11. The final image shows a deep blue in the water and a bright blue for the sky.

Hue/Saturation

The Hue/Saturation dialog box lets you rotate the image's hue, saturation, and lightness/darkness. You can apply this effect to the whole image, or just a selection. If you don't like the color of the outfit you're wearing, it's pretty easy to change.

Hue changes the color, from red to blue, for example.

Saturation changes how intense the color is. A color with more saturation looks more colorful, with less gray in it.

Lightness is how bright a color is. The brighter a color, the more it will lean towards white.

To change a color in a selection:

1. Open the file you want to change (**Figure 9**).

2. Click the Advanced button.

3. Using the Color Wand select the portion of the image you want to change.

   We selected both the water and sky.

4. Click the Quality tab.

5. Click the Hue/Saturation button.

   This brings up the Hue/Saturation dialog box where you can adjust the Hue, Saturation, and Lightness (**Figure 10**).

6. Drag the sliders to modify the selected area.

   In our example, we dragged the Hue slider towards the right and the Saturation slider to 80 for more saturation. This changed the water to a deep rich blue and the sky to a bright blue.

7. Click the OK button.

   The selected areas will be modified using the values you entered (**Figure 11**).

Variations

Variations gives you multiple previews of your selection (or entire image if no portion is selected) in both its current state and how it will appear if you modify it in in one of several ways. You can think of it as a Color Balance with a little less control, but one that is easier to use.

To use Variations on an image:

1. Open the image you want to adjust (Figure 12).

2. Click the Advanced button.

3. Click the Quality tab.

4. Click the Variations button.

    This activates the Variations dialog box (**Figure 13**). You can add yellow, red, magenta, blue, cyan, or green.

5. If the image is too red, add more cyan and green to balance out the red overtones, as in this image.

6. Click the OK button to see the final results (**Figure 14**).

    When using Vairations, keep in mind that if you click on each color once, you're back to where you started. Each color has an opposite color across from it in the Variations dialog box.

Figure 12. The original photo has intense red/magenta overtones.

Figure 13. The Variations dialog box lets you balance the color.

Figure 14. The final image shows an even range of colors.

Intellihance Pro 4 folder on HD
Not mention in Plug-ins folder
161408

81171

Mr M Scott
31 Beech Avenue
Chichester
W Sussex
PO19 3DR

DOLLOND *&* **AITCHISON**
The Opticians
76/77 North Street,
Chichester,
Sussex, PO19 1LQ.

Tel: 01243 789927

PLEASE NOTE NEW ADDRESS

January 1999

06092   026709

Dear Mr Scott,

Half Price Frame Sale... Plus Your Extra 10% Saving

We recently wrote to remind you that your eye examination was due. If you still have to make the appointment please call to book one today and make sure you don't miss out on D&A's Half Price Frame Sale*.

Figure 15. The initial setup window for installing Intellihance.

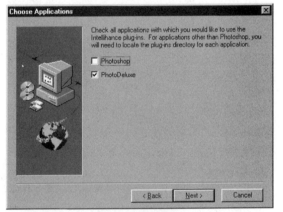

Figure 16. Choose PhotoDeluxe as your linked application.

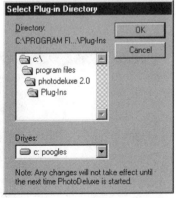

Figure 17. Be sure to select the correct plug-ins folder/directory.

PhotoDeluxe can use third-party plug-ins to give you more effects to work with. Extensis makes a great plug-in called Intellihance 3.0. Intellihance is an image correction plug-in that gives you many controls at one time to fix your image.

To install Intellihance 3.0 in Windows 95:

1. Quit PhotoDeluxe if it is running.

2. Put the Extensis CD in the CD-ROM drive.

3. Double-click the My Computer icon.

4. Double-click the Extensis CD in the [D] drive.

5. Double-click the ihance3 folder.

6. Double-click the Us_setup folder.

7. Double-click the setup icon (Figure 15).

8. Follow the instructions and be sure to check whether you want to install for Photoshop or PhotoDeluxe (Figure 16).

9. When done, click the OK button.

10. After launching PhotoDeluxe be sure to choose File⇨Preferences⇨Plug-Ins to activate the Select Plug-in Directory dialog box (Figure 17).

11. Click the Plug-Ins folder and then click the OK button.

To install Intellihance 3.0 for Macintosh:

1. Double-click on the Extensis CD-ROM.

2. Double-click on the Install Intellihance 3.0 icon.

3. When prompted, select PhotoDeluxe 2.0 as the application for Intellihance to install to.

Installing Intellihance

163

To use Extensis' Intellihance 3.0 to enhance an image in PhotoDeluxe:

1. Open the image that needs to be adjusted (Figure 18).

2. Click the Advanced button.

   This also activates all of the pull-down menus.

3. Choose Effects⇨Extensis⇨ Intellihance 3.0.(Figure 19).

   Intellihance has three areas to explore. You can click the Enhance Image button and let Intellihance figure it out. You can click the Preferences button and access more functions, allowing you to customize exactly how Intellihance will work with images. Finally, you can click the Fine Tune button (in Preferences) and apply your own specific settings to any one image.

4. Click the Enhance Image button (Figure 20).

   The Enhance Image button will adjust the image to what Intellihance thinks would look best (Figure 21).

Figure 18. The original image is cloudy and unclear.

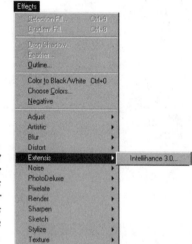

Figure 19. The Intellihance plug-in is found under the Effects pull-down menu.

Figure 21. The final image is beautiful with no work on your part.

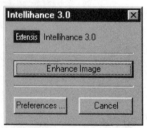

Figure 20. The main Intellihance dialog box is easy to use, with one button to do all the work.

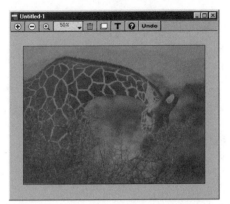

Figure 22. The original image is underdeveloped.

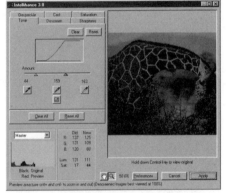

Figure 23. The Fine Tune area gives you many more choices to fix your image.

Figure 24. The final image is stunning.

Intellihance's built-in Fine Tune controls allow you to use specific image adjustment settings in combination with the "intelligent enhancement" that Intellihance normally uses. This is a great way to get a specific image looking just right.

To use Intellihance Fine Tune:

1. Open the image that needs to be adjusted (Figure 22).

2. Choose Effects⇨Extensis⇨ Intellihance 3.0.

3. Click the Preferences button.

4. Click the Fine Tune button.

   This opens the Fine Tune dialog box that give you more control than the presets in the Preferences dialog box. Here you can fine tune the Despeckle, Cast, Saturation, Tone, Descreen, and Sharpness. The eyedroppers are quite handy for fixing your image.

5. In the Tone tab, drag the three sliders above the eyedroppers until your image looks good in the preview window (Figure 23).

   The left slider controls the darkest point (moving it to the left darkens the image, but makes the darkest areas more like black). The right slider controls the lightest areas (moving it to the right lightens the image and makes the lightest areas white). The middle slider is the 50% mark; moving this slider to the left lightens the image, while moving it to the right darkens the image.

6. If necessary, click the other tabs to clean up your image even more.

7. Click the Apply button to accept the new changes (Figure 24).

Color correction is a subjective process. What looks good to one person may look terrible to another. Intellihance allows you to customize the way Intellihance works each time you click the Enhance button.

To set Intellihance's Preferences:

1. Open the image that needs to be adjusted (Figure 25).

2. Click the Advanced button.

3. Choose Effects⇨Extensis⇨ Intellihance 3.0.

4. Click the Preferences button.

   This brings up a dialog box (**Figure 26**). You can adjust the Descreen, Contrast, Brightness, Saturation, Cast, Sharpness, and Despeckle. Within each of these settings, you have between four and six pop-up choices. By holding down the Ctrl (Control) key, you can see what the image looks like before Intellihance corrected it.

5. Click the Apply button to see the final changes (Figure 27).

Figure 25. The original image is underdeveloped.

Figure 26. The Intellihance dialog box gives you a preview of your changes.

Figure 27. The final image is brighter and clearer.

PAINTING

ONE thing that most people don't realize about PhotoDeluxe is that you can do some pretty amazing *painterly* things with the software.

By using the Brush tool, or one of the other tools, you can add all sorts of paint effects to images, or create brand new images just by painting.

Painting Tools

PhotoDeluxe has six tools that you can use to create painterly effects. You can work with the Brush, Line, Eraser, Smudge, and Clone tools. Color Change lets you change the foreground and background colors.

To use the Brush tool to create movement:

1. Open the image you want to brush (Figure 1).

2. Click the Advanced button.

3. Click the Tools tab.

4. Click the Brush tool.

   This opens the Brushes dialog box (**Figure 2**). Here you can choose the type of brush, size of brush, and the paint color. The two types of brushes are a hard-edged and a soft-edged brush.

5. Choose a small soft-edged brush.

6. Change the color to white by clicking on the Color button in the Brushes dialog box and then clicking on the top area of the color ramp to pick a white color.

7. Click the OK button.

8. Zoom in close enough to see where you want to brush.

9. Using the mouse, gently sweep the brush to simulate movement (Figure 3).

The Painting Tools

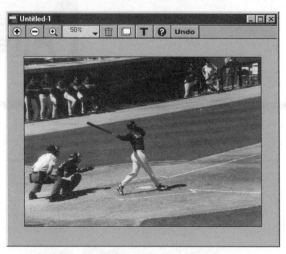

Figure 1. We'd like to see this swing show some real movement.

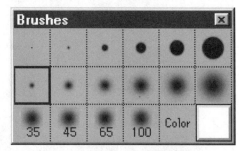

Figure 2. You have sixteen brushes to choose from.

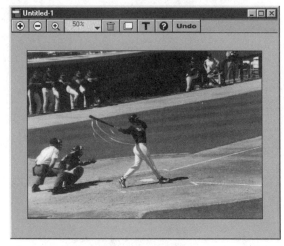

Figure 3. It is almost like you're there and seeing the hit.

Figure 4. This picture shows a basic office.

Figure 5. You can change the size and color of the line with ease. Lines, lines, everywhere lines.

Figure 6. The complete office is labeled.

To use the Line tool for placing labels on photos:

1. Open the image you want to label (Figure 4).

2. Click the Advanced button.

3. Click the Tools tab.

4. Click the Line button.

   This brings up the Line Tool Options dialog box, where you can choose the line width and the color.

5. Click the Color button in the Line Tool Options dialog box to change the line color.

6. Click and drag a line (Figure 5).

7. To add text, click the T icon to access the Type dialog box. p118

8. Add the labels to finish the image (Figure 6).

Using the Line Tool to Create Labels

To use the Eraser tool:

1. Open the image you want to erase (Figure 7).

2. Click the Advanced button.

3. Click the Tools tab.

4. Click the Eraser button.

   This brings up the Erasers dialog box (**Figure 8**). Here you choose the size and type of brush.

5. Click on a medium brush with a soft edge.

6. Carefully click or click and drag around the edge of the object you want to keep to erase the background (Figure 9).

   The Eraser tool works great to eliminate a background and soften the edge. If your background isn't easily selected, you can erase to white, and use the Color Wand to select later.

Figure 7. We'd like to eliminate this background.

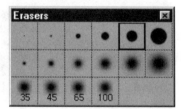

Figure 8. The soft edge brush works nicely to remove the background and leave a softened edge.

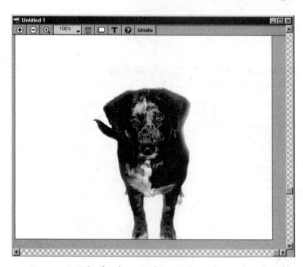

Figure 9. The background is ready to be replaced or the object can now easily be selected.

Figure 10. The food on the table can be emphasized by smudging the background.

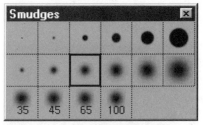

Figure 11. The Smudges dialog box lets you choose the size and style of brush.

Figure 12. Smudging the background really brings out the foreground.

To use the Smudge tool to blur a background:

1. Open the image to be smudged (Figure 10).

2. Click the Advanced button.

3. Click the Tools tab.

4. Click the Smudge tool.

   This brings up the Smudges dialog box (**Figure 11**). Choose the size and type of brush to smudge with.

5. Choose a large brush to smudge areas further away from the food and a smaller brush to hone in closer to the food (Figure 12).

   We like the soft edge brush for a more natural look.

Smudging with the Smudge Tool

To clone away parts of an image:

1. Open the image you want to clone (Figure 13).

2. Click the Advanced button.

3. Click the Tools tab.

4. Click the Clone button.

   This accesses the Clone dialog box (**Figure 14**). Here you can choose the size and style of brush you want to use.

5. Move the crosshairs to the part of the image you want to copy and click.

   This sets the source for the Cloning process.

6. Click and drag in a different location to "paint" with the source area.

   We chose to remove the sign and electrical lines so you can see the stormy sky (**Figure 15**).

7. Move the cloning crosshairs to the saguaro and duplicate the cactus (Figure 16).

Figure 13. The original has some annoying elements that we'd like to remove.

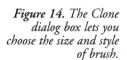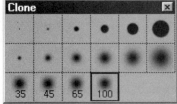

Figure 14. The Clone dialog box lets you choose the size and style of brush.

Figure 16. We added a couple of cactus sentries to make the scene more like the desert.

Figure 15. The offending signs and power lines are gone.

Figure 17. The original cathedral is beautiful, but we don't need to see the whole image.

Figure 18. The Feather dialog box lets you choose what section you want to fill or get rid of.

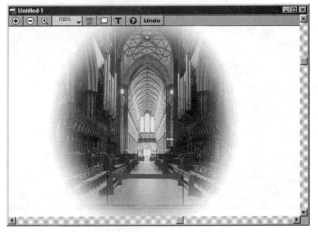

Figure 19. The feathered effect creates a beautiful soft photo.

To feather an image:

1. Open the image that you want to feather (Figure 17).

2. Click the Advanced button.

3. Show the Selections dialog box by choosing View⊏>Show Selections.

4. Choose the Oval Tool.

5. Click and drag an oval around the area you want to keep.

6. Click the Effects tab.

7. Click the Feather button.

   This opens the Feather dialog box (**Figure 18**). You can select how much of a feather you want, the fill color, and the action. The Action area lets you delete the selection, delete the background, fill the selection, or fill the background.

8. Click the OK button to see the wonderful results (Figure 19).

Feathering Out a Background

TIPS & TECHNIQUES

The higher the number of pixels specified in the Feather dialog box, the softer the edge will be.

To use the outline effect to create a painterly look:

1. Open the image you want to outline (Figure 20).

2. Click the Advanced button.

3. Within the image, select the object you want to outline using any Selection tool.

   We used the SmartSelect tool to select the car.

4. Click the Effects tab.

5. Click the Outline button.

   This activates the Outline dialog box (**Figure 21**). You choose the width, location, blending, and the color of the outline.

6. Click the OK button to see the yellow outline on the car (Figure 22).

Figure 20. Let's add a neon glow to this car.

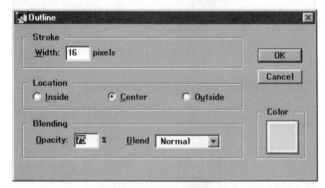

Figure 21. The Outline dialog box lets you choose the thickness, location, and the opacity of the line.

Figure 22. With a snazzy radioactive-looking glow, this car looks like it came straight from Middletown, PA.

Outlining Objects

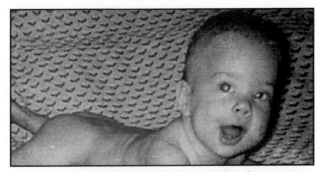

Figure 23. This cute baby is a perfect candidate for painting.

Figure 24. The pink in the cheeks gives a rosy glow.

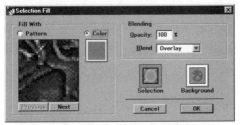

Figure 25. The Selection Fill dialog box.

Figure 26. The final image has a soft natural quality.

To paint a black and white photo:

1. Open the black and white photo (Figure 23).

2. Click the Advanced button.

3. Click the Tools tab.

4. Click the Brush button.

   This opens the Brushes dialog box.

5. Choose a soft brush and a color to paint with.

6. Paint the cheeks with a hint of blush.

7. Click the Smudge button.

   The Smudges dialog box appears.

8. Choose a soft brush and soften the edges of the color on the cheeks (Figure 24).

9. Select the background using the Trace tool.

10. Click the Effects tab.

11. Click the Selection Fill button to open the Selection Fill dialog box (Figure 25).

12. Choose the Color button and the color you want to use.

13. Choose the Opacity and the Blend type.

    We chose Overlay so you can still see the texture of the blanket underneath.

14. Click the Selection button so that the fill is applied to the Selection, not the background.

15. Click the OK button to see the results (Figure 26).

    Since this page is only black and white, the difference is harder to see than in color (the lighter areas shown in the figures are the painted areas). A similar effect is shown in the color pages of this book.

Painting a Black and White Photo

SPECIAL EFFECTS AND FILTERS

ALL sorts of special effects are available through PhotoDeluxe. Filters are used to achieve most of these effects.

PhotoDeluxe has several different classes of filters, from artistic filters to distortion filters. Throughout this chapter, we've displayed original images and the effects you can achieve using most of the filters available in PhotoDeluxe.

This chapter shows you what most of the filters do, and some of the fascinating effects you can create with them. Some of these effects are similar to ones found in other places in PhotoDeluxe, but the Filter menu is the primary location to start exploring when you need some fantastic effect applied to an image.

Artistic

The Artistic filters include: Crystallize, Find Edges, Mezzotint, Mosaic, Pointillize, and Posterize. When applying these effects, you tend to get a more artsy result. With the exception of Find Edges, all of the other effects open up a dialog box. In the dialog box, you can use a mini preview to adjust the settings to your tastes.

Crystallize

The Crystallize special effect changes your image (**Figure 1**) into a bunch of polygons (**Figure 3**). You determine the size of the polygons in the Crystallize dialog box (**Figure 2**). These polygons resemble a honeycomb. The color of the polygon is determined by the predominate colors in the cell size chosen. The lower the cell size, the more you'll retain of your original image. The higher the cell size, the less you'll retain of your image. The high settings result in colorful-looking glass shards.

Try using Crystallize after you have added Noise to a plain background. This will make a larger texture that you can lighten and put in as a backdrop for text or another image.

Figure 1. The original image consists of bright jellybeans.

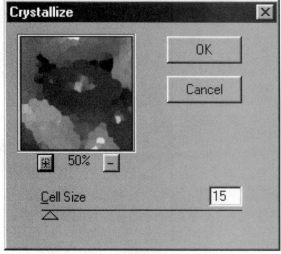

Figure 2. The Crystallize dialog box lets you control the size of the crystals that will be created.

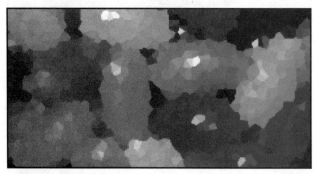

Figure 3. The jellybeans have an erratic and edgy look to them.

Figure 4. This lovely view of the arch looks like it came straight out of an art history book.

Find Edges

The Find Edges effect has no dialog box. That means the effect is simply applied with no input on your part. Find Edges will add a colored outline effect to your selection. The edges are colored on a white background. This effect works wonderfully on images that have a good amount of contrast (**Figure 4**). After applying Find Edges to the selection, you see a definite lined edge (**Figure 5**).

Figure 5. The Find Edges effect completely changes the look of this image to an artist's rendering of an architectural scene.

Finding the Edges of an Image

TIPS & TECHNIQUES

If you want to create a more defined edge, first pump up the contrast. To increase the contrast, click the Advanced button, click the Quality tab, and click the Brightness/Contrast button. Here you can adjust either the brightness, contrast, or both. When you increase the contrast, you'll define a stronger edge for the Find Edges effect. This effect is also very useful in tracing a section or the whole image.

Mezzotint

The Mezzotint effect attempts to create a halftone pattern using dots, lines, or strokes. A halftone pattern changes your image from a photo-like quality to a dotted artsy look. This effect tends to come off a tad harsh rather than as a softened dotted look. You can apply the effect to the whole or part of your image.

We took an original landscape and created a rectangular selection with the Rectangle tool. Then, by clicking the Invert button in the Selections dialog box, a frame-like selection was made (**Figure 6**). In the Mezzotint dialog box, you have ten choices for how the effect will be applied (**Figure 7**).

The Mezzotint dialog box also has a preview screen so you can see how each of the ten choices will look before you click the OK button. The final mezzotint frame really sets off this landscape (**Figure 8**).

Mezzotint can be softened afterwards using the Soften effect. Sometimes even the smallest mezzotint setting can still look too harsh.

Figure 6. The lake image would look great in some sort of frame.

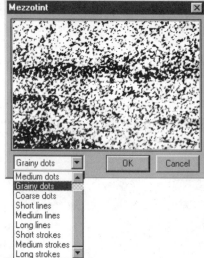

Figure 7. The Mezzotint dialog box offers ten choices (only nine are showing).

Figure 8. The Mezzotint effect creates a frame for the photo.

Figure 9. The original basketball court image.

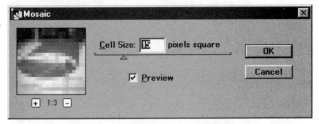

Figure 10. The Mosaic dialog box lets you choose the cell size and whether or not you want to see a preview.

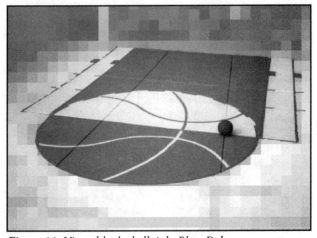

Figure 11. Virtual basketball, à la PhotoDeluxe.

Mosaic

The Mosaic effect lets you change the size of the pixels. An image is made up of pixels (dots) on your screen. When you hear the term ppi (pixels per inch) that refers to how many of these pixels are contained in one square inch. The more pixels per inch, the more detailed your image will look. The mosaic effect lets you choose a larger cell size or how many pixels per square inch.

The image in **Figure 9** shows a basketball court scanned in from a photo. In the Mosaic dialog box (**Figure 10**) you set the cell size. If the Preview box is checked, you can see the effect of the cell size before you click the OK button. The larger the cell size, the larger the squares. The smaller the cell size, the smaller the squares will be for the mosaic. We created a selection around the background except the key area of the basketball court. After applying the Mosaic effect, a blocky blurry image is added to the background (**Figure 11**).

Using the Mosaic Filter

Pointillize

The Pointillize effect creates an impressionistic result on your selection. It creates dots based on the cell size that you choose in the Pointillize dialog box. The larger dots seem to create a worm-like effect. The smaller dots resemble Seurat-like paintings. This effect can add a lovely painterly look to your entire image or just part of it.

In **Figure 12**, we selected just the background, and not the skeleton in the foreground. In the Pointillize dialog box (**Figure 13**), a cell size of 8 was used. The final effect shows a painterly texturized background and a clear image of the skeleton in the foreground (**Figure 14**).

The Pointillize effect not only creates dots based on the entered cell size, but it also fills in the color you have chosen for your background color behind the dots. In **Figure 15**, we changed the background color to white to see how that would look; we like the darkened version better.

Figure 12. The original image shows Jen after working too many hours on this book.

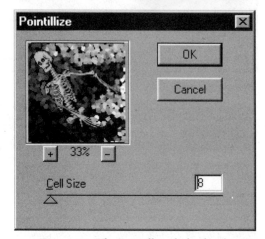

Figure 13. The Pointillize dialog box lets you choose the size of the dots or cells.

TIPS & TECHNIQUES

You can change the background color by choosing Effects⇨Choose Colors from the pull-down menus. This brings up the Color Picker dialog box. If you click on the background swatch, you'll activate that swatch. Now, by dragging the eyedropper over a color you want, the active swatch (background) will be filled with that new color. You can also double-click the swatch to activate the Color window to choose some basic colors, or create your own custom colors.

Figure 14. The textured background has black filled in behind the dots.

Figure 15. The white background behind the dots makes this image harder to see.

Using Pointillize

Figure 16. Sam is hiding among his imaginary friends.

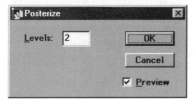

Figure 17. In the Posterize dialog box, a lower number creates a more dramatic and colorful effect.

Posterize

Posterizing an image lets you determine the brightness of an image and retain as much color in the image as you want. The Posterize effect will break down the image into the number of levels you enter. The levels also determine how much color is retained. The higher the number you enter, the more colors and light, midtone, and dark tones will be retained. The lower the number you enter, the fewer light, midtone, and dark tones will be retained.

Figure 16 shows one real animal amidst several stuffed ones. This image is rich in colors, so it is perfect to show some of the effects of using Posterize. In the Posterize dialog box (**Figure 17**) we have entered a low number to see how this will affect the whole image (**Figure 18**). When you enter a higher number such as 8, the effect has less contrast (**Figure 19**).

Figure 18. The low setting of 2 shows only four colors and four different levels of brightness.

Figure 19. The higher setting of 8 still shows some banding stripes between colors.

Posterizing Images

183

Fun

The effects that fall under the Fun tab let you have a blast with your whole image or just a piece of it. You have seven effects to choose from: Pinch, Ripple, Shear, Sphere, Twirl, Pond Ripple, and Negative. Each effect creates a distortion on your selection.

Pinch

The Pinch effect works best when you select a piece of your image (using any of the selection tools). When you drag the slider in the Pinch dialog box to the right (positive numbers) the image is squished inward. By dragging the slider in the Pinch dialog box to the left (negative numbers) you bulge out your selection. We call this the Jimmy Durante effect.

We love using the Pinch effect on people or animals because of the fun results. Ted offered his own face for practicing the Pinch effect (**Figure 20**). In the Pinch dialog box (**Figure 21**), you see a small preview of the effect before clicking the OK button. If you drag the Amount slider to the right, you'll get a pinched or pulled-in effect (**Figure 22**). If you drag the Amount slider to the left, you'll get a bulged-out effect (**Figure 23**).

The Pinch effect is wonderful for changing just a nose or the eyes of a person. Let's think of it as a preview to plastic surgery. By creating a selection around each eye, you can bulge the eyes out in surprise.

Figure 20. What a smug-looking photo of Ted. Let's see how a little plastic surgery would look on him.

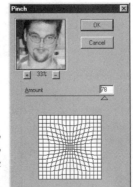

Figure 21. The Pinch dialog box lets you pinch inward or bulge outward a whole image or selection.

Figure 22. The Pinch setting set high gives Ted a "squished" look.

Figure 23. The Pinch setting set in the opposite direction gives Ted that dopey look.

Figure 24. This poor horse looks trapped in this background.

Ripple

The Ripple effect distorts your selection by creating waves. You choose whether the waves are small, medium, or large. The higher you drag the Amount slider, the wavier the effect. A great way to create a textured background is to select only the background and apply the Ripple effect. The higher the setting, the more dramatic the ripple. If you want a slight ripple, enter a lower amount in the Ripple dialog box.

The background of this stunning horse was selected for a ripple effect (**Figure 24**). In the Ripple dialog box, you can see a preview, and set the amount and size of the ripple waves (**Figure 25**). After the Ripple effect is applied, the background looks glassy (**Figure 26**).

The Ripple effect is also used to create a marble texture. The higher the setting, the more marbelized the texture becomes.

Figure 25. The Ripple dialog box lets you choose the amount and size of the ripples.

Figure 26. The new rippled background frees Murphy from the chain restraints.

Rippling Images

Shear

The Shear effect distorts an image vertically. In the Shear dialog box (**Figure 27**), you can drag the top and bottom points to create a sheared or wavy effect. The dialog box has a preview window so you can see exactly how the effect will look before you click the OK button.

You can apply the Shear effect in a straight angled manner, or a warped wavy manner. If you click and drag the top point to the right and the bottom point to the left, then the whole image slants to the right (**Figure 28**). Clicking on the middle of the line and dragging a curve creates a wavy effect rather than a straight angled effect (**Figure 29**).

The two options you have in the Undefined Areas section of the dialog box are to Wrap Around or Repeat Edge Pixels. If you choose Wrap Around, the image will repeat itself. If you choose Repeat Edge Pixels, then the outside pixel colors will repeat those colors.

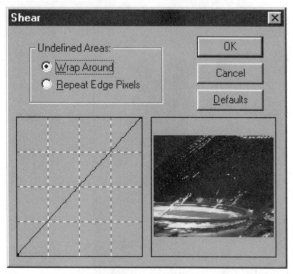

Figure 27. The Shear dialog box lets you choose whether to angle or wave the image.

Figure 28. This image was sheared to the right slightly.

Figure 29. A curved line in the Shear dialog box produced this wavy effect.

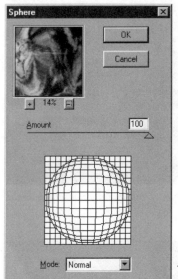

Figure 30. The Sphere dialog box lets you choose a bloated or squished effect.

Sphere

The Sphere effect puts your selection around a ball shape. Sphere may seem like the Pinch effect. In essence they do a very similar thing, but the Amount slider is dragged in opposite directions. To create a bulged effect with the Sphere effect, drag the slider to the right. To create a bulged effect with the Pinch effect, drag the slider to the left. To create a pinched in effect with the Sphere effect, drag the slider to the left. To get the same effect with the Pinch effect, drag the slider to the right.

The Sphere dialog box (**Figure 30**) lets you choose between a bloated effect or a squished-in effect. The cat in **Figure 31** is perfect for creating a sphere effect on only a selected portion of a the image. In the Sphere dialog box, keep the Amount at 100 to get a bulged effect (**Figure 32**). If you want a squished effect, drag the Amount slider to -100 (**Figure 33**).

Applying Sphere to Images

Figure 31. Static is a fine feline specimen.

Figure 32. Static becomes feline-eggus headus.

Figure 33. Static the rabbit.

Cool and Cooler

The Cool and Cooler tabs let you add wacky effects to your whole image or just a part of it. There are seven cool effects to choose from: Page Curl, Chalk & Charcoal, Merge Clouds, Chrome, Neon Glow, Patchwork, and Funnel. The Cooler tab has seven effects: Colored Pencil, Bas Relief, Note Paper, Crackle, Solarize, Sponge, and Emboss. A few of the effects will be grayscale, even on color images.

Page Curl

The Page Curl effect will make your image look like it is peeling off the page. The effect is quite three-dimensional. The actual curl is transparent and the page underneath will reflect the foreground color you have chosen.

This picture of Ken looks just like any photograph, flat and two dimensional (**Figure 34**). When you click the Page Curl button, the effect will be created instantly, without the usual dialog box.(**Figure 35**).

Figure 34. Ken is happy, but awfully two-dimensional.

Figure 35. With the peel of a page, we can release Ken into the three-dimensional world.

Curling Page Corners

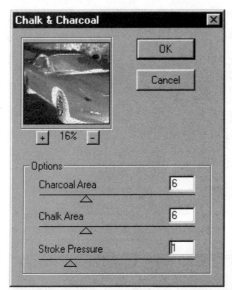

Figure 36. The Chalk & Charcoal dialog box lets you set the pressure, and chalk and charcoal area, as well as see a small preview.

Chalk & Charcoal

The Chalk & Charcoal effect turns your image or selection into a charcoal drawing. This artistic effect changes any color image to black and white. In the Chalk & Charcoal dialog box (**Figure 36**) you set the Charcoal area, the Chalk area, and the Stroke Pressure.

If you drag the Charcoal area slider to zero, then the image will be rendered in chalk. If you drag the Chalk Area to zero, then the image will be rendered in charcoal. To create an even chalk and charcoal image, set both areas to the same number. If you use a heavy stroke pressure, the image will be rendered darker and with more contrast (**Figure 37**). If you enter a low number, then the image will be rendered lightly and will appear very gray (**Figure 38**).

Try experimenting with only one of the Charcoal or Chalk settings by making the other setting zero.

Figure 37. Using a heavy stroke produces an image that has sharp contrasts and lines.

Figure 38. This chalky image resembles the original car.

Applying a Chalk & Charcoal Effect

Funnel

The Funnel effect will create a rectangular to polar, or polar to rectangular effect. Rectangular to Polar wraps the edges of an image together to form a circular image. If you choose Polar to Rectangular, then the effect will take an image and stretch it out (imagine taking the surface of a globe off and stretching it to form a rectangle). The image of the arch (**Figure 39**) looks great when you apply the Funnel effect, Rectangular to Polar (**Figure 40**). The same image creates a double arch (no, not McDonald's) from the original image (**Figure 41**).

This effect is great to use with an image that has text. It will round the text if you choose rectangular to polar.

Figure 39. The original image: a beautiful work of architecture.

Figure 40. Rectangular to Polar results in a spaceship or arch.

Figure 41. Polar to Rectangular creates a double image.

Funneling Images

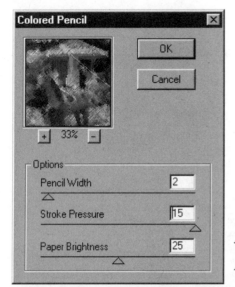

Figure 42. The Colored Pencil dialog box lets you choose how heavy a colored pencil will be used.

Colored Pencil

The Colored Pencil effect gives you a beautiful pencil drawn look. The Colored Pencil dialog box lets you choose the Pencil Width, Stroke Pressure, and Paper Brightness (**Figure 42**). This effect is quite delicate and artistic.

The original garden picture is beautiful, but can be made to look quite painterly (**Figure 43**). The heavier the pencil width, the less detail will be retained because the pencil is larger. If you choose a light stroke pressure, the image will have little to no contrast and appear as one blobby color. The heavier the stroke pressure, the more contrast and detail will be brought out (**Figure 44**).

The Paper Brightness set to a low number will create a whiter image. The higher the setting, the more color will be brought out.

Using the Colored Pencil effect will make any of your photos look more like paintings.

Figure 43. The original image is a lovely garden picture.

Figure 44. The Colored Pencil effect gives a soft look to this garden.

Using the Colored Pencil Filter

Crackle

The Crackle effect makes your image or selection look as if it is printed on a textured paper. You can make the effect more three-dimensional by increasing the Crack spacing, depth, and brightness in the Crackle dialog box (**Figure 45**). This effect is great for creating a strong texture. The original image is quite colorful and is a great example for the Crackle effect (**Figure 46**). After applying the effect, the image looks as if it was printed on a textured paper (**Figure 47**).

Imagine the Crackle effect as printing on crinkled paper. The Crack spacing determines how much space is between the individual cracks. The Crack Depth can pop-out the cracks when set to a high amount. The Crack Brightness will also make the cracks more three-dimensional.

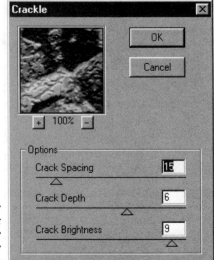

Figure 45. The Crackle dialog box let you choose the intensity of the cracks.

Applying a Crackle Texture

Figure 46. This happy family shot is actually a group of actors posing to look like a family for a top-secret goverment agency.

Figure 47. The family picture now looks like it was processed on crinkled paper, even though the original image was much less than perfect.

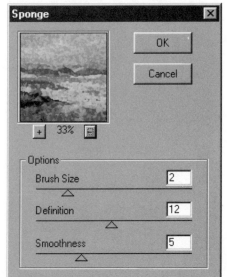

Figure 48. The Sponge dialog box soaks up any errors you have ever made in PhotoDeluxe.

Sponge

Another painterly look is created by using the Sponge effect. This effect looks as if someone painted your photo using a sponge. You determine the brush size, definition, and smoothness in the Sponge dialog box (**Figure 48**).

The higher the Brush Size, the less detail you'll retain. When set to a high number, the Definition slider will retain more detail. When set lower, the Definition slider will retain less definition in the image. If the Smoothness slider is set to a high value, it will create a blurry look. A low smoothness will create a crisper look.

The lake landscape can easily be turned into a painting (**Figure 49**). After applying the Sponge effect, the picture looks painted (**Figure 50**). This is a great way to make your photos into "paintings." Then all you have to do is have them printed and framed for your walls.

The Sponge effect doesn't work with images that need to retain detail. It softens the image and creates an impressionistic look.

Brush Size is the size of the brush used in the painterly effect. The larger the brush, the less detail will be in the resulting image.

Definition is the amount of contrast between the brush areas. The more definition, the "clearer" the image will appear to be.

Smoothness controls how blurry the edges of the brush strokes will be. The higher the setting, the less obvious the strokes themselves.

Figure 49. The lake picture is an inspiration for any painter.

Figure 50. It's amazing that with a click of a button, your dream to be a painter becomes a reality.

Using Sponge

GLOSSARY

Anti-aliasing The process used to simulate soft diagonal and curved edges in pixel-based images.

Bitmap An image that consists of only black and white pixels, with no values in between. Also a common way of referring to pixel-based images.

Blur To defocus an area, removing contrast and sharpness by blending colors together smoothly, reducing definition.

Brightness The lightness of a pixel. The lighter the pixel, the whiter it becomes.

Cast A color that appears over an image, usually unwanted.

Colorspace How the image is made, from either CMYK colors or RGB colors.

CMYK Short for Cyan, Magenta, Yellow, and Black. CMYK colors are used for printing full-color images.

Continuous Tone An original photograph or negative.

Contrast The amount of difference between adjoining colors.

Feathering Partially selecting pixels along the edge of a selection. The higher the feather amount, the more pixels will be partially selected.

Filter A PhotoDeluxe feature that modifies an image or a selection.

GIF89a A type of image format limited to 256 colors. GIF89a images can contain transparent areas and image map information, making them suitable for use on web pages.

Grayscale An image that consists of black, white, and gray pixels.

JPEG A type of image format, commonly used on the World Wide Web due to its small file size. Short for Joint Photographic Experts Group.

Moiré An unwanted pattern that appears when process color screens are not aligned properly in the printing process.

Noise Light or dark specks that appear in an image.

Photoshop Adobe's high-end photo manipulation software, with many of the same features found in PhotoDeluxe.

PICT A common file type found on the Macintosh, short for Picture.

Pixel An individual square of color within an image. A typical image has thousands of pixels.

Process Colors A set of colors that make up a full-color image. Typically these colors are cyan, magenta, yellow, and black.

Resolution The number of pixels in an inch, measured both horizontally and vertically. An image can have a resolution of 72 ppi (pixels per inch), which means that there are 72 pixels going across and down each inch.

RGB Red, Green, and Blue. The three colors used by scanners when an image is scanned in, and when an image is displayed on screen.

Saturation The intensity of color in any pixel. The less saturated, the more gray the pixel will appear.

Scanning The process of bringing a photograph into the computer. Most personal scanners are *flatbed* scanners, where a photograph is placed face down on a glass surface.

Selection The active area within an image. When a portion of an image is selected, only that portion will be affected by most PhotoDeluxe functions.

Sharpness The opposite of blurriness. The sharper the image, the crisper and more defined it is.

TIFF A common image file format used for printing images. Short for Tagged Image File Format.

INDEX

squares
    alternate key combinations for
        drawing, 51
    creating square selections, 51
Start menu (Windows 95), 6
Status Bar, 15
storing
    images for easy retrieval, 74
    photos on CD, 11
stucco textures, 140
swapping backgrounds, 124
swirl textures, 136-137

T

tabs, for advanced interface, 58
templates
    for business cards, 129
    for calendars, 36
    for certificates, 133
    for covers, 38
    for gift tags, 39
    for labels, 128
    for signs, 132
    for stationery designs, 130
Templates dialog box, 36
text
    adding to images, 118
    brightening sections for, 102
    creating textured backgrounds
        for, 138-139
    layers and, 116
Text Tool dialog box
    entering text for envelopes, 131
    illustrated, 38
textured backgrounds, 153
textured buttons
    creating, 90-91
    exporting to Web pages, 92
textures and 3D effects, 135-146
    creating
        depth, 145, 146
        with mezzotint, 180
        shadows, 89, 91, 142-143
        shocked effects, 141
        a stucco texture, 140
        a swirl texture, 136-137

textures for text
    backgrounds, 138-139
    curling up corner of photo, 144, 188
    using Crackle effect, 140, 192
TIFF files, 70, 82, 83
TIFF Options dialog box, 82, 127
toolbar, 16
tools
    choosing from Selections palette, 45
    choosing Selection tools from menu, 59
    painting, 168-172
    selecting directory for, 17
    selection, 46-56
    See also specific tools listed by name
Tools tab (Advanced button), cloning
    images, 62
Touch Up tab (Get Photo button), 23
touching up images, 23, 97-113
    adding
        noise for background
            textures, 105-106
        a wind effect, 108-109
    adjusting
        brightness/contrast, 28, 102,
            160, 179
        color balance of an image, 101
        red eye, 26, 98
    changing eye color, 99
    combining effects for, 111, 112-113
    creating a circular effect, 107
    with Instant Fix, 28-29, 100
    removing dust or scratches, 110
    sharpening blurry images, 103
    See also softening
Trace tool
    creating free-form selections with, 49
    defined, 46
tracing
    with SmartSelect tool, 30
    with Trace tool, 49
transformation box, 47
trimming images, 72
T-shirt transfers
    creating, 40
    printing and exporting, 81
T-Shirts Templates, 40
Twirl dialog box, 137
Typical Setup (Windows 95), 4

Index S-T

Index U-W

MACINTOSH SHORTCUTS

Adobe PhotoDeluxe 2

Function	Keyboard Shortcut
New Document	Command-N
Open Document	Command-O
Open Clip Art	Command-\
Close Document	Command-W
Save Document	Command-S
Send Document to Hold Photo	Command-H
Print Preview	Command-/
Print	Command-P
Cursor Preferences	Command-K
Quit	Command-Q
Undo	Command-Z
Cut	Command-X
Copy	Command-C
Paste	Command-V
Duplicate	Command-;
Select All	Command-A
Select None (deselect)	Command-D
Invert Selection	Command-I
Trace Selection Tool	Command-L
Rectangle Selection Tool	Command-M
Color Wand	Command-F
Move Tool	Command-G
Show/Hide Brushes Palette	Command-J
Display Text Dialog Box	Command-T
Rotate Left	Command-<
Rotate Right	Command->
Free Rotate	Command-4
Flip Horizontal	Command-[
Flip Vertical	Command-]

Function	Keyboard Shortcut
Eraser	Command-E
Resize	Command-6
Trim	Command-7
Distort	Command-2
Perspective	Command-5
Instant Fix	Command-3
Color Balance	Command-Y
Brightness/Contrast	Command-B
Hue/Saturation	Command-U
Sharpen	Command-1
Selection Fill	Command-9
Gradient Fill	Command-8
Color to Black/White	Command-0
Hide Rulers	Command-R
Zoom In	Command-+
Zoom Out	Command-—
Constrain to Straight Line while Painting	Shift
Opacity Setting 100%	0
Opacity Settings 10%-90%	1-9
Fill with Foreground Color	Delete
Fill with Background Color	Option-Delete
Nudge Selection 1 Pixel	Arrow Keys
Nudge Selection 10 Pixels	Shift-Arrow Keys
Hand Tool	Spacebar
Zoom In Tool	Command-Spacebar
Zoom Out Tool	Command-Option-Spacebar
Temporary Move Tool	Command
Constrain Movement to 45° Angles	Shift
Don't Constrain Size to 1:1 Ratio	Shift

Macintosh Shortcuts

WINDOWS SHORTCUTS

Adobe PhotoDeluxe 2

Function	Keyboard Shortcut
New Document	Ctrl+N
Open Document	Ctrl+O
Open Clip Art	Ctrl+\
Close Document	Ctrl+W
Save Document	Ctrl+S
Send Document to Hold Photo	Ctrl+H
Print Preview	Ctrl+/
Print	Ctrl+P
Cursor Preferences	Ctrl+K
Quit	Ctrl+Q
Undo	Ctrl+Z
Cut	Ctrl+X
Copy	Ctrl+C
Paste	Ctrl+V
Duplicate	Ctrl+;
Select All	Ctrl+A
Select None (deselect)	Ctrl+D
Invert Selection	Ctrl+I
Trace Selection Tool	Ctrl+L
Rectangle Selection Tool	Ctrl+M
Color Wand	Ctrl+F
Move Tool	Ctrl+G
Show/Hide Brushes Palette	Ctrl+J
Display Text Dialog Box	Ctrl+T
Rotate Left	Ctrl+<
Rotate Right	Ctrl+>
Free Rotate	Ctrl+4
Flip Horizontal	Ctrl+[
Flip Vertical	Ctrl+]

Function	Keyboard Shortcut
Eraser	Ctrl+E
Resize	Ctrl+6
Trim	Ctrl+7
Distort	Ctrl+2
Perspective	Ctrl+5
Instant Fix	Ctrl+3
Color Balance	Ctrl+Y
Brightness/Contrast	Ctrl+B
Hue/Saturation	Ctrl+U
Sharpen	Ctrl+1
Selection Fill	Ctrl+9
Gradient Fill	Ctrl+8
Color to Black/White	Ctrl+0
Hide Rulers	Ctrl+R
Zoom In	Ctrl++
Zoom Out	Ctrl+−
Constrain to Straight Line while Painting	Shift
Opacity Setting 100%	0
Opacity Settings 10%-90%	1-9
Fill with Foreground Color	Delete
Fill with Background Color	Alt+Delete
Nudge Selection 1 Pixel	Arrow Keys
Nudge Selection 10 Pixels	Shift+Arrow Keys
Hand Tool	Spacebar
Zoom In Tool	Ctrl+Spacebar
Zoom Out Tool	Ctrl+Alt+Spacebar
Temporary Move Tool	Ctrl
Constrain Movement to 45° Angles	Shift
Don't Constrain Size to 1:1 Ratio	Shift